Workshop on Information Extraction and Knowledge Acquisition 2011

(IEKA 2011)

Held with the 8th International Conference on Recent Advances in Natural Language Processing 2011 (RANLP 2011)

Hissar, Bulgaria
16 September 2011

ISBN: 978-1-62276-460-0

Printed from e-media with permission by:

Curran Associates, Inc.
57 Morehouse Lane
Red Hook, NY 12571

Some format issues inherent in the e-media version may also appear in this print version.

Printed by Curran Associates, Inc. (2012)

Association for Computational Linguistics
209 N. Eighth Street
Stroudsburg, Pennsylvania 18360

Phone: 1-570-476-8006
Fax: 1-570-476-0860

acl@aclweb.org

Additional copies of this publication are available from:

Curran Associates, Inc.
57 Morehouse Lane
Red Hook, NY 12571 USA
Phone: 845-758-0400
Fax: 845-758-2634
Email: curran@proceedings.com
Web: www.proceedings.com

Preface

The RANLP 2011 Workshop on *Information Extraction and Knowledge Acquisition* (IEKA 2011) took place on September 16, 2011 in Hissar, Bulgaria, following the conference on Recent Advances in Natural Language Processing (RANLP 2011).

The workshop was envisioned as a meeting place for those concerned with the fields of information extractions (IE) and knowledge acquisition (KA). Until a decade ago, these fields were mostly limited to identifying and extracting named entities, semantic and ontological relations, events, templates, and facts in relatively small text corpora using a small variety of external resources such as gazetteers, thesauri, and lexical hierarchies.

Today everything has changed. The size of corpora has grown dramatically: using Gigaword-scale data is common, and it is almost standard to use the Web, which contains quadrillions of words, or at least the Google Web 1T 5-grams. More importantly, new types of communication have emerged, such as chats, blogs and, in the last 2-3 years, Twitter, whose informal language poses many challenges to automatic IE and KA, yet they are becoming increasingly important, e.g., for learning customer opinions on various products and services. Social network analysis is another emerging topic, where data is naturally much more interconnected than in the rest of the Web.

All these recent developments have posed not only new challenges, but have also created a number of opportunities, opening new research directions, and offering new useful resources. For example, the growth of Wikipedia has given rise to DBpedia and other collaboratively-created resources such as Freebase. Today, IE and KA researchers can even create annotations and resources on demand as they need them for a very low price using crowd-sourcing tools such as Amazon's Mechanical Turk.

We received 12 submissions, and, given our limited capacity as a one-day workshop, we were only able to accept seven full papers for oral presentation: an acceptance rate of 58%. The workshop also featured two invited talks (by Ralph Grishman and by Ralf Steinberger), and a panel discussion (involving Kevin Cohen, Georgi Georgiev, Petya Osenova, Elena Paskaleva, and Kiril Simov).

We would like to thank the members of the Program Committee for their timely reviews. We would also like to thank the authors for their valuable contributions.

Preslav Nakov, Zornitsa Kozareva, Kuzman Ganchev, Jerry Hobbs
Co-Organizers

Organizers:

Preslav Nakov, National University of Singapore
Zornitsa Kozareva, University of Southern California
Kuzman Ganchev, Google Inc.
Jerry Hobbs, University of Southern California

Program Committee:

Javier Artiles, Queens College
Kalina Bontcheva, University of Sheffield
Razvan Bunescu, Ohio State University
Hamish Cunningham, University of Sheffield
Mona Diab, Columbia University
Greg Druck, University of Massachusetts Amherst
Georgi Georgiev, Ontotext AD
Filip Ginter, University of Turku
Jennifer Gillenwater, University of Pennsylvania
Andrew Gordon, USC/ICT
João Graça, University of Pennsylvania
Chikara Hashimoto, NICT
Nitin Indurkhya, eBay
Hagen Fürstenau, Saarland University
Alex Kulesza, University of Pennsylvania
Maussam, University of Washington
Su Nam Kim, The University of Melbourne
Alexandre Klementiev, Johns Hopkins University
Ana-Maria Popescu, Yahoo!
Ryan McDonald, Google
Andrés Montoyo, University of Alicante
Rafael Muñoz, University of Alicante
Roberto Navigli, University of Rome
Manuel Palomar, University of Alicante
Siddharth Patwardhan, IBM
Marco Pennacchiotti, Yahoo!
Simone Paolo Ponzetto, University of Heidelberg
Sampo Pyysalo, University of Tokyo
Sujith Ravi, ISI, University of Southern California
Ellen Riloff, University of Utah
Alan Ritter, University of Washington
Paolo Rosso, Technical University of Valencia
Kenji Sagae, USC/ICT
Thamar Solorio, University of Alabama at Birmingham
Ralf Steinberger, JRC
Mihai Surdeanu, Stanford University
Idan Szpektor, Yahoo! Research
Valentin Tablan, University of Sheffield
Jörg Tiedemann, University of Uppsala
Ivan Titov, Saarland University
Aline Villavicencio, Federal University of Rio Grande do Sul
Alexander Yates, Temple University

Additional Reviewers:

Gabor Angeli

Invited Speakers:

Ralph Grishman, New York University
Ralf Steinberger, European Commission Joint Research Centre

Panelists:

Kevin Cohen, University of Colorado, School of Medicine
Georgi Georgiev, Ontotext AD
Petya Osenova, Bulgarian Academy of Sciences
Elena Paskaleva, Bulgarian Academy of Sciences
Kiril Simov, Bulgarian Academy of Sciences

Table of Contents

Workshop Program

Friday: September 16, 2011

09:00–09:05 **Welcome**

Session I

09:05–10:05 **Invited Talk 1**
The Knowledge Base Population Task: Challenges for Information Extraction
Ralph Grishman, New York University

10:05–10:30 *Fine-grained Entity Set Refinement with User Feedback*
Bonan Min and Ralph Grishman

10:30–11:00 **BREAK**

Session II

11:00–11:25 *Extraction of Domain-specific Opinion Words for Similar Domains*
Ilia Chetviorkin and Natalia Loukachevitch

11:25–11:50 *The Role of Predicates in Opinion Holder Extraction*
Michael Wiegand and Dietrich Klakow

11:50–12:15 *Dependency-Based Text Compression for Semantic Relation Extraction*
Marcos Garcia and Pablo Gamallo

12:15–14:15 **LUNCH**

Session III

14:15–14:40 *How to Distinguish a Kidney Theft from a Death Car? Experiments in Clustering Urban-Legend Texts*
Roman Grundkiewicz and Filip Graliński

14:40–15:05 *Machine Reading Between the Lines: A Simple Evaluation Framework for Extracted Knowledge Bases*
Avirup Sil and Alexander Yates

15:05–15:30 *Temporal Expressions Extraction in SMS messages*
Stéphanie Weiser, Louis-Amélie Cougnon and Patrick Watrin

15:30–16:00 **BREAK**

Friday: September 16, 2011 (continued)

Session IV

16:00–17:00 **Invited Talk 2**
Bringing Multilingual Information Extraction to the User
Ralf Steinberger, European Commission Joint Research Centre

17:00–18:00 **Panel**

Moderator: Preslav Nakov

Panelists:
- Kevin Cohen, University of Colorado, School of Medicine
- Georgi Georgiev, Ontotext AD
- Petya Osenova, Bulgarian Academy of Sciences
- Elena Pakaleva, Bulgarian Academy of Sciences
- Kiril Simov, Bulgarian Academy of Sciences

18:00–18:05 **Closing Remarks**

The Knowledge Base Population Task: Challenges for Information Extraction (invited talk)

Ralph Grishman
New York University
grishman@cs.nyu.edu

Abstract

The Knowledge Base Population (KBP) task, being run for the past 3 years by the U.S. National Institute of Standards and Technology, is the latest in a series of multi-site evaluations of information extraction, following in the tradition of MUC and ACE. We examine the structure of KBP, emphasizing the basic shift from sentence-by-sentence and document-by-document evaluation to corpus-based extraction and the challenges it raises for cross-sentence and cross-document processing. We consider the problems raised by the limited amount and incompleteness of the training data, and how this has been (partly) addressed through such methods as semi-supervised learning and distant supervision. We describe some of the optional tasks which have been included – rapid task adaptation (last year), temporal analysis (this year), cross-lingual extraction (planned for next year) – and others which have been suggested.

Proceedings of the Workshop on Information Extraction and Knowledge Acquisition, page 1,
Hissar, Bulgaria, 16 September 2011.

Fine-grained Entity Set Refinement with User Feedback

Bonan Min
New York University
715 Broadway, 7th floor
New York, NY 10003 USA
min@cs.nyu.edu

Ralph Grishman
New York University
715 Broadway, 7th floor
New York, NY 10003 USA
grishman@cs.nyu.edu

Abstract

State of the art semi-supervised entity set expansion algorithms produce noisy results, which need to be refined manually. Sets expanded for intended fine-grained concepts are especially noisy because these concepts are not well represented by the limited number of seeds. Such sets are usually incorrectly expanded to contain elements of a more general concept. We show that fine-grained control is necessary for refining such sets and propose an algorithm which uses both positive and negative user feedback for iterative refinement. Experimental results show that it improves the quality of fine-grained sets significantly.

1 Introduction

Entity set expansion is a well-studied problem with several techniques proposed (Bunescu and Mooney 2004, Etzioni et al. 2005, Wang and Cohen 2007, Sarmento et al. 2007, Pasca 2007, Pasca 2004, Pantel et al. 2009, Pantel and Lin 2002, Vickrey et al. 2010). In practice, semi-supervised methods are preferred since they require only a handful of seeds and are more flexible for growing various types of entity sets. However, they usually produce noisy sets, which need to be refined (Vyas and Pantel, 2009). Fine-grained sets such as *National Capitals* are particularly noisy. Such concepts are intrinsically hard because they're not well represented by initial seeds. Moreover, most related instances have a limited number of features, thus making it hard to retrieve them.

We examined a few sets expanded for fine-grained concepts and observed that lots of erroneous expansions are elements of a more general concept, whose sense overlaps and subsumes the intended sense. For example, the concept *National Capitals* is expanded to contain *Major cities*. In such cases, a proposed feature-pruning technique using user-tagged expansion errors to refine sets (Vyas and Pantel 2009) removes some informative features of the target concept. Moreover, since refining such sets needs more information about the target concept, it is natural to use user-tagged correct expansions as well for the refinement.

In this paper, we refer to the problem of fine-grained concepts being erroneously extended as *semantic spread*. We show that a rich feature representation of the target concept, coupled with appropriate weighting of features, is necessary for reducing *semantic spread* when refining fine-grained sets. We propose an algorithm using relevance feedback, including both positive and negative user feedback, for set refinement. By expanding the set of features and weighting them appropriately, our algorithm is able to retrieve more related instances and provide better ranking. Experimental results show that it improves the quality of fine-grained sets significantly.

2 Related work

There is a large body of research on growing named entity sets from a handful of seeds. Some are pattern-based algorithms. Sarmento et al. (2007) uses explicit patterns, e.g. *"...NE_a, NE_b and NE_c..."*, to find named entities of the same class. Pasca (2004) uses the pattern *<[StartOfSent] X [such as|including] N [and|,|.]>* (Hearst 1992) to find instances and their class labels from web logs. Some are based on distributional similarity. The distributional hypothesis states that similar terms tend to appear with similar contexts (Harris 1954). For example, Pasca (2007) extracts templates (prefixes and suffixes around seeds) from search engine query logs as features, and then ranks new instances by their similarity with the seeds in the vector space of pattern features for growing sets. Their method

Proceedings of the Workshop on Information Extraction and Knowledge Acquisition, pages 2–6,
Hissar, Bulgaria, 16 September 2011.

outperforms methods based on handcrafted patterns (Pasca 2004) but requires extensive query logs to tolerate noisy queries. Calculating the similarity matrix between all pairs of named entities is expensive. Pantel et.al (2009) proposed a web-scale parallel implementation on the MapReduce distributed computing framework.

Observing the low quality of expanded sets, Vyas and Pantel (2009) uses negative user feedback for set refinement. They propose the Similarity Method (SIM) and Feature Modification Method (FMM), to refine entity sets by removing expansions which are similar to user-tagged errors, and removing features related to the erroneous sense from the centroid of the seed set for better ranking, respectively. Their algorithms rely on two assumptions 1) most expansion errors are caused by ambiguous seeds, and 2) entities which are similar in one sense are usually not similar in their other senses. They show average performance gain over a few sets. Vyas et al. (2009) studied the problem from the other side by selecting better seeds. They proposed three metrics and three corresponding algorithms to guide editors to choose better seeds. All three algorithms outperform the baseline.

3 Similarity modeling revisited

Given a set of candidate named entities represented by vectors of features, the goal of set refinement is to find a subset of entities which are similar to the target concept, based on a certain similarity metric (Cosine, Dice, etc). The concept is usually approximated with a set of seed instances. A previous feature pruning technique (Vyas and Pantel 2009) aims at reducing semantic drift introduced by ambiguous seeds.

We're particularly interested in fine-grained classes since they're intrinsically hard to expand because of the crude representation from the limited number of seeds. In practice, we observed, when expanding fine-grained classes, that *semantic spread* instead of semantic drift (McIntosh 2010) severely affects expansion quality. By *semantic spread* we mean a situation where an initial concept, represented by its member entities, changes in the course of entity set expansion into a broader concept which subsumes the original concept.

Semantic spread is usually introduced when erroneous instances, which belong to a more general concept, are incorrectly included during the set expansion process. For example, when using Google Sets (labs.google.com/sets) to expand *National Capitals*, we found a highly ranked error *New York*. By checking with our distributional thesaurus extracted from 37 years' newspaper, we notice the following features: *prep_in(embassy, *)* [1], *nn(*, capital)*, *nn (*, president)*. These are indicators of capital cities. However, as the financial "capital" and a politically important city, *New York* shares lots of informative features with the *National Capitals* concept. Therefore, we need more sophisticated techniques for the refinement process for fine-grained concepts.

4 Refine fine-grained classes with user feedback

User feedback is a valuable resource for learning the target concept. We propose to use both positive and negative feedback to learn a rich set of features for the target concept while weighting them appropriately. Our algorithm chooses informative instances to query the user, uses positive feedback for expanding the feature set, and negative feedback for feature weight adjustment.

Relevance feedback (Harman 1992) is widely applied to improve search engine performance by modifying queries based on user feedback. Various techniques are proposed for both the vector space model and probabilistic model. Since set refinement is done in the vector space of features, we only consider techniques for the vector space model. To refine entity sets, the centroid of all vectors of seeds is used as a query for retrieving related named entities from the candidate pool. Observing that errors are usually caused by incorrect or overweighted features of seeds, we propose to incorporate user feedback for set refinement with a variant of the Rocchio algorithm (Rocchio 1971). The new centroid is calculated as follows:

$$Centroid = \frac{\sum_{I \in S \cup P} I}{|S \cup P|} - \gamma \cdot \frac{\sum_{C_N \in N} C_N}{|N|}$$

where I is an entity that is a member of seed set S or the set of user-tagged positive entities P, and C_N is a member of the set of user-tagged negative entities N. γ is the parameter penalizing features of irrelevant entities. This method does feature set expansion and iterative adjustment of feature weights for the centroid. It adds features from informative instances back into the centroid

[1] Syntactic context is used in our experiment. For the format of dependencies, please refer to the Stanford typed dependencies manual.

and penalizes inaccurate features based on user-tagged errors, thus modifying the centroid to be a better representation of the target class.

4.1 Query strategy

To be practical, we should ask the user to review as few instances as possible, while obtaining as much information as possible. Observing that 1) top-ranked instances are likely to be positive 2) random instances of a fine-grained class usually contain relatively few features with non-zero weight, thus not providing much information for approaching the target concept, our procedure selects at each iteration the *n* instances most similar to the centroid and presents them to the user in descending order of their number of features with non-zero weight (the user will review higher-dimension ones first). This ranking strategy prefers more representative instances with more features (Shen et al., 2004). The user is asked to pick the first positive instance.

A similar idea applies to negative instance finding. We use co-testing (Muslea et al., 2006) to construct two ranking-based classifiers on randomly split views of the feature space. Instances are ranked by their similarity to the centroid. The classifiers classify instances which ranked higher than the golden set size as correct, and classify others as incorrect. We select *n* contention instances – instances identified as correct expansions by one of the classifiers and incorrect by the other. These instances are more ambiguous and likely to be negative. Instances are also presented to the user in descending order of number of features with non-zero weight. Coupled with the strategy for positive instance finding, it helps to reweight a rich set of features.

Since we asked the user to review instances that are most likely to be positive and negative, and these instances are presented to the user in sequence, the user only has to review very few examples to find a positive and a negative instance in each iteration. In practice we set *n*=10. We observed that around 85% of the time the user only has to review 1 instance to find a correct one, and over 90% of the time has to review 3 or fewer instances to find a negative one.

5 Experiment

Corpus: we used 37 years newspaper corpus[2] which is dependency parsed with the Stanford Parser[3] and has all named entities tagged with Jet[4] NE tagger (we didn't use the NE tags reported by the tagger but only the fact that it is a name). We use syntactic context, which is the grammatical relation in conjunction with the words as feature, and we replace the word in the candidate NE with *. Both syntactic contexts in which the candidate entities are the heads and contexts in which the candidate entities are the dependents are used. The feature set is created from syntactic contexts of all entities tagged in the corpus. An example common feature for class National Capital is prep_in(ministry, *). We remove features in which the dependent is a stop word, and remove a limited number of less useful dependency types such as numerical modifier and determiner. We use pointwise mutual information (PMI) to weight features for entities, and cosine as the similarity measure between the centroid of the seeds and candidate instances. PMI scores are generated from the newspaper corpus statistics. Candidates are then ranked by similarity. We construct each named entity candidate pool by including similar instances with cosine score greater than 0.05 with the centroid of the corresponding golden set. This ensures that each candidate pool contains tens of thousands of elements so that it contains all similar instances with high probability.

Golden sets[5]: Several golden sets are prepared by hand. We start from lists from Wikipedia, and then manually refine the sets[6] by removing incorrect instances and adding correct instances found as distributionally-similar instances from the corpus. The criteria for choosing the lists is 1) our corpus covers most elements of the list, 2) the list represents a fine-grained concept, 3) it contains hundreds of elements for reasons of fairness, since we don't want the added positive examples themselves to overshadow other aspects of the evaluated algorithms. Based on these criteria, we chose three lists: *National Capitals, IT companies*[7] and *New York City (NYC) neighborhoods*. All three sets have more than 200 elements. User feedback is simulated by checking membership in the golden set. Since existing

[2] It contains news articles from: TDT5, NYT(94-00), APW(98-00), XINHUA(96-00), WSJ(94-96), LATWP(94-97), REUFF(94-96), REUTE(94-96), and WSJSF(87-94). It contains roughly 65 million sentences and 1.3 billion tokens.

[3] http://nlp.stanford.edu/software/lex-parser.shtml

[4] http://cs.nyu.edu/grishman/jet/license.html

[5] Golden sets are available for download at http://www.cs.nyu.edu/~min/goldset_37news.tgz

[6] Manually checking indicates the golden sets are complete with high probability.

[7] Set contains both software and hardware companies

golden sets such as the sets from Vyas and Pantel (2009) are not designed specifically for evaluating refinement on fine-grained concepts and they are quite small for evaluating positive feedback (with less than 70 elements after removing low frequency ones in our corpus), we decided to construct our own.

Algorithms evaluated: The following algorithms are applied for iteratively updating the centroid using user-tagged examples: 1) **baseline algorithm (BS),** an algorithm adding the correct example most similar to the centroid as a new seed for each iteration; this simulates using the user-tagged first positive example to assist refinement, 2) **RF-P**, relevance feedback algorithm using only positive feedback by adding one informative instance (selected using the method described in section 4.1) into seed set, 3) **FMM** (Vyas and Pantel, 2009) which uses the first user-tagged negative example for feature pruning in each iteration. 4) **RF-N**, relevance feedback algorithm using only negative feedback (selected using the method described in section 4.1), 5) Relevance feedback (**RF-all**) using both positive and negative user feedback selected using methods from Section 4.1. We use 6 seeds for all experiments, and set γ=0.25 for all RF experiments.

For each algorithm, we evaluate the results after each iteration as follows: we calculate a centroid feature vector and then rank all candidates based on their similarity to the centroid. We add sufficient top-ranked candidates to the seed and user-tagged positive items to form a set equal in size to the golden set. This set, the *refined set*, is then compared to the golden set. The following tables show a commonly reported metric, average R-precision[8] of 40 runs starting with randomly picked initial seeds (The first column shows the number of iterations.):

	BS	RF-P	FMM	RF-N	RF-all
2	0.258	0.298	0.253	0.246	0.286
4	0.260	0.317	0.250	0.251	0.316
6	0.260	0.323	0.244	0.255	0.332
8	0.260	0.325	0.243	0.255	0.342
10	0.265	0.325	0.245	0.256	0.343

Table 1. Performance on class *national capitals*

	BS	RF-P	FMM	RF-N	RF-all
2	0.303	0.340	0.301	0.303	0.319
4	0.312	0.403	0.303	0.311	0.406
6	0.317	0.432	0.312	0.312	0.451
8	0.323	0.442	0.312	0.314	0.467
10	0.327	0.445	0.306	0.314	0.481

Table 2. Performance on class *IT companies*

	BS	RF-P	FMM	RF-N	RF-all
2	0.168	0.190	0.159	0.161	0.191
4	0.179	0.217	0.164	0.163	0.232
6	0.189	0.235	0.163	0.166	0.249
8	0.198	0.243	0.166	0.176	0.259
10	0.206	0.248	0.169	0.181	0.262

Table 3. Performance on class *NYC neighborhoods*

Results show that RF-P outperforms the baseline algorithm by using positive examples with rich contexts rather than the first positive example for each iteration. The baseline algorithm shows small improvement over 10 iterations. This shows that simply adding the example which is most similar to the centroid is not very helpful. Comparing R-precision gain between RF-P and the baseline suggests that selecting informative examples is critical for refining fine-grained sets. By enriching the feature set of the centroid, RF-P is able to retrieve instances with a limited number of features overlapping the original centroid. RF-N outperforms FMM since it only reweights (penalizes some weights) but doesn't prune out intersection features between user-tagged errors and the centroid. This flexibility avoids over-penalizing weak but informative features of the intended concept. For FMM, we observe a small performance gain with successive iterations over *IT companies* and *NYC neighborhoods* but a performance decrease for *National Capitals*. Inspection of results shows that FMM tends to retrieve more *capital cities* for small geographical regions because of removal of weak features for informative sense such as *Major Cities*.

Combining RF-P and RF-N, RF-all uses both positive informative examples and negative informative examples to expand feature sets of the centroid and weight them appropriately, thus achieving the most performance gain. RF-N by itself doesn't improve performance significantly. Comparing RF-all with RF-P, using informative negative examples helps to improve performance substantially because only when both informative positive examples and informative negative examples are used can we learn a significantly large set of features and appropriate weights for them.

[8] Precision at the rank of golden set size

We also implemented a few methods combining positive feedback and FMM, and didn't observe encouraging performance. RF-all also has the highest Average Precision (AP) for all sets, thus showing that it provides better ranking over candidates. Due to space limitations, tables of AP are not included. The quality of the top ranked elements with RF-all can be seen in the precision at rank 50 for the three sets: 84.6%, 81.6%, and 71.7%.

6 Conclusion and Future work

We propose an algorithm using both positive and negative user feedback to reduce semantic spread for fine-grained entity set refinement. Our experimental results show performance improvement over baseline and existing solutions.

Our next step is to investigate feature clustering techniques since we observe that data sparseness severely affects set refinement.

Acknowledgments

We are grateful to the anonymous reviewers for their valuable comments. We would like to also thank Prof. Satoshi Sekine and Ang Sun for their helpful discussion and comments on an early draft of this paper.

References

Razvan Bunescu and Raymond J. Mooney. 2004. Collective Information Extraction with Relational Markov Networks. In Proceedings of ACL-04.

Oren Etzioni, Michael Cafarella, Doug Downey, Ana-Maria Popescu, Tal Shaked, Stephen Soderland, Daniel S. Weld and Alexander Yates. 2005. Unsupervised named-entity extraction from the Web: An Experimental Study. In Artificial Intelligence, 165(1):91-134.

Donna Harman. 1992. Relevance feedback revisited. In Proceedings of SIGIR-92.

Zellig S. Harris. 1954. Distributional Structure. Word. Vol 10: 146-162.

Marti A. Hearst. 1992. Automatic acquisition of hyponyms from large text corpora. In Proceedings of COLING-92.

Tara McIntosh. 2010. Unsupervised discovery of negative categories in lexicon bootstrapping, In Proceedings of EMNLP-10.

Ion Muslea, Steven Minton and Craig A. Knoblock. 2006. Active Learning with Multiple Views, Journal of Artificial Intelligence Research 27: 203-233.

Patrick Pantel, Eric Crestan, Arkady Borkovsky, Ana-Maria Popescu and Vishnu Vyas. 2009. Web-Scale Distributional Similarity and Entity Set Expansion. In Proceedings of EMNLP-09.

Patrick Pantel and Dekang Lin. 2002. Discovering word senses from text. In Proceedings of KDD-02.

Marius Pasca. 2004. Acquisition of Categorized Named Entities for Web Search, In Proceedings of CIKM-04.

Marius Pasca. 2007. Weakly-supervised discovery of named entities using web search queries. In Proceedings of CIKM-07.

Marco Pennacchiotti and Patrick Pantel. 2009. Entity Extraction via Ensemble Semantics. In Proceedings of EMNLP-09.

J. J. Rocchio. 1971. Relevance feedback in information retrieval. The SMART Retrieval System: Experiments in Automatic Document Processing: 313-323.

Luis Sarmento, Valentin Jijkoun, Maarten de Rijke and Eugenio Oliveira. 2007. "More like these": growing entity classes from seeds. In Proceedings of CIKM-07.

Dan Shen, Jie Zhang, Jian Su, Guodong Zhou and Chew-Lim Tan. 2004. Multi-criteria-based active learning for named entity recognition. In Proceedings of ACL-04.

David Vickrey, Oscar Kipersztok and Daphne Koller. 2010. An Active Learning Approach to Finding Related Terms. In Proceedings of ACL-10.

Vishnu Vyas and Patrick Pantel. 2009. Semi-Automatic Entity Set Refinement. In Proceedings of NAACL/HLT-09.

Vishnu Vyas, Patrick Pantel and Eric Crestan. 2009, Helping Editors Choose Better Seed Sets for Entity Set Expansion, In Proceedings of CIKM-09.

Richard C. Wang and William W. Cohen. 2007. Language- Independent Set Expansion of Named Entities Using the Web. In Proceedings of ICDM-07.

Extraction of Domain-specific Opinion Words for Similar Domains

Ilia Chetviorkin
Faculty of Computational Mathematics and Cybernetics, Lomonosov Moscow State University
ilia2010@yandex.ru

Natalia Loukachevitch
Research Computing Center Lomonosov Moscow State University
louk_nat@mail.ru

Abstract

In this paper we consider a new approach for domain-specific opinion word extraction in Russian. We suppose that some domains have similar sentiment lexicons and utilize this fact to build an opinion word vocabulary for a group of domains. We train our model in movie domain and then utilize it to book and game domains. Obtained word list quality is comparable with quality of initial domain list.

1 Introduction

The web is full of customers' opinions on various products. Automatic extraction, processing and summarization of such opinions are very useful for future users. Opinions about products are often expressed using evaluative words and phrases that have a certain positive or negative sentiment. Therefore, important features in the qualitative classification of opinions about a particular entity are opinion words and expressions used in the domain. The problem is that it is impossible to compile a list of opinion expressions, which will be equally applicable to all domains, as some opinion phrases are used only in a specific domain while the others are context-oriented [Lu et. al., 2011]. Indeed, sentiment lexicons adapted to a particular domain or topic have been shown to improve task performance in a number of applications, including opinion retrieval [Jijkoun et. al., 2010], and expression-level sentiment classification [Choi and Cardie, 2009]. In addition there are several studies about context-dependent opinion expressions [Lu et. al., 2011].

The number of different domains is very large, and recent studies are focused on cross-domain approaches, to bridge the gap between the domains [Pan et al, 2010]. On the other side there are different subject fields that has similar sentiment lexicon. For example: «breathtaking» is an opinion word in entertainment (movies, books, games etc.) domain, but non-opinion in the politics domain. At the opposite side some words («evil», «treachery» etc.) have strong sentiment in politics domain, but are neutral in entertainment domain, these words do not express any opinion about a film, game or book.

Thus we suppose that different domains can be separated into clusters (for example: entertainment, digital goods, politics, traveling etc.) where domains of the same cluster have similar sentiment lexicons.

In this paper we focus on the problem of construction of a domain-specific sentiment lexicon in Russian, which can be utilized for various similar domains.

We present a new supervised method for domain-specific opinion word extraction. We train this method in one domain and then utilize it in two others. Then we combine extracted word lists to construct a general list of opinion words typical to this domain cluster.

Our approach is based on several text collections, which can be automatically formed for many subject areas. The set of text collections includes: a collection of product reviews with author evaluation scores, a text collection of product descriptions and a contrast corpus (for example, a general news collection). For each word in a review collection we calculate various statistical features using aforementioned collections and then apply machine learning algorithms for term classification.

To evaluate the effectiveness of the proposed method we conduct experiments on data sets in three different domains: movies, books and computer games. The results show that our approach can identify new opinion words specific to the given domain (for example "fabricated" in movie domain).

For further evaluation of the lexicon quality, we manually labeled extracted word lists, and our method is proved to be effective in construct-

Proceedings of the Workshop on Information Extraction and Knowledge Acquisition, pages 7–12,
Hissar, Bulgaria, 16 September 2011.

ing a qualitative list of domain-dependent sentiment lexicon. The results also demonstrate the advantage of combining multiple lists of opinion words over using any single list.

The reminder of this article is organized as follows. In Section 2 we describe the state-of-the-art in the opinion words extraction sphere, Section 3 describes our approach in the movie domain, in Section 4 we utilize our approach for two other domains and combine opinion word vocabularies for all three domains.

2 Related Work

Sentiment lexicon plays an important role in most, if not all, sentiment analysis applications, including opinion retrieval, opinion question answering and summarization, opinion mining [Ding et. al., 2008]. Even though supervised machine learning techniques have been shown to be effective for sentiment classification task [Pang and Lee, 2008], authors in [Choi and Cardie, 2009] demonstrate that including features from sentiment lexicons boosts classification performance significantly.

Generally there are three main approaches to the automatic identification of opinion words in texts.

The first approach is manual labeling, which is very labor-intensive and error-prone process. In addition the coverage of this approach is usually very low.

The second approach is based on information from a dictionary or a thesaurus. In this approach a small initial set of words is usually chosen manually, and then expanded with the help of dictionaries and thesaurus entries. The basic principle of this approach is that if a word has sentiment polarity, then its synonyms and antonyms have polarity too (orientation may change). Therefore, from the initial set of words, a new, more complete set of opinion words can be constructed [Hu and Liu, 2004, Neviarouskaya et.al., 2009]. In [Esuli and Sebastiani, 2005], dictionary definitions are used for opinion words extraction. The basic idea is that words with the same orientation have "similar" glosses.

The third approach – corpus-based training. This approach is based on finding rules and patterns in the texts [Kanayama and Nasukawa, 2006]. In [Turney, 2002] word polarity is calculated by comparing the co-occurrence statistics of various words with words "excellent" and "poor". Authors assume that words with similar semantic orientation tend to co-occur. The resulting opinion orientation of the words is used to classify reviews to positive and negative.

There are some works that combine second and third approaches [Ding et. al., 2008]. More importantly, although existing works try to learn opinion words in a specific domain, few of them directly evaluate the quality of the generated lexicon.

3 Proposed method

In this section we will describe our method in respect to movie domain. We will train the model on the movie data and then try to utilize it in other domains.

3.1 Data Preparation

We collected 28773 film reviews of various genres from online recommendation service *www.imhonet.ru*. For each review, user's score on a ten-point scale was extracted. We called this collection the **review collection**.

Example of the movie review:

Nice and light comedy. There is something to laugh - exactly over the humor, rather than over the stupidity... Allows you to relax and gives rest to your head.

We also needed a contrast collection of texts for our experiments. In this collection the concentration of opinions should be as little as possible. For this purpose, we had collected 17680 movie descriptions. This collection was named **description collection**.

One more contrast corpus was a collection of one million news documents. We had calculated document frequency of each word in this collection and used only this frequency list further. This list was named **news corpus**.

3.2 Collections with Higher Concentration of Opinions

We suggested that it was possible to extract some fragments of the reviews from review collection, which had higher concentration of opinion words. These fragments include:

- Sentences ending with a «!»;
- Sentences ending with a «…»;
- Short sentences, no more than 7 word length;
- Sentences containing the word «movie» without any other nouns.

We call this collection – **small collection**.

3.3 Statistical Features

Our task was to create a qualitative list of opinion words based on the calculation of various features. We used the following set of features for each word:

- Frequency of the word in the collection (i.e. number of occurences in all documents in the collection)
- The number of documents where the word occurs
- Weirdness
- TFIDF
- Deviation from the average score
- Word score variance
- Frequency of capitalized words

We will consider some of them in more detail.

Weirdness. To calculate this feature two collections are required: one with high concentration of opinion words and the other – contrast one. The main idea of this feature is that opinion words will be «strange» in the contexts of the contrast collection. This feature is calculated as follows [Ahmad et. al, 1999]:

$$\text{Weirdness} = \frac{w_s / t_s}{w_g / t_g}$$

where w_s – frequency of the word in special corpus, t_s – total count of words in special corpus, w_g – frequency of the word in general corpus, t_g – total count of words in general corpus. Instead of frequency one can use the number of documents where the word occurs.

TFIDF. There are many varieties of this feature. We used TFIDF variant described in [Callan et. al., 1992] (based on BM25 function):

$$\text{TFIDF} = \beta + (1-\beta)\cdot tf \cdot idf$$

$$tf_D(l) = \frac{\text{freq}_D(l)}{\text{freq}_D(l) + 0.5 + 1.5 \cdot \frac{dl_D}{\text{avg\_dl}}}$$

$$idf(l) = \frac{\log\left(\frac{|c| + 0.5}{df(l)}\right)}{\log(|c| + 1)}$$

freq(l) – number of occurrences of l in a document (collection),

dl(l) – length measure of a document,

avg_dl – average length of a document,

df(l) – number of documents in a collection (e.g. movie descriptions, news collection) where term l appears,

$\beta = 0.4$ by default,

$|c|$ – total number of documents in a collection.

Deviation from the average score. As we mentioned above we had collected user's numerical score (on a ten point scale) for each review. The main idea of this feature is to calculate average score for each word (sum of review ratings where this word occurs divided into their number) in the collection and then subtract average score of all reviews in the collection from it.

$$dev(l) = \left|\frac{\sum_{i=1}^{n} m_i k_i}{k} - \frac{\sum_{i=1}^{n} m_i}{n}\right|$$

$$\sum_{i=1}^{n} k_i = k$$

where l – considered lemma, n – total count of the reviews in the collection, m_i – i-th review score, k_i – frequency of the lemma in the i-th review (may be 0).

Word score variance. Using review ratings we can calculate the score variance for each word. This feature can show us how often a word is used in reviews with significantly different scores. If a word has small deviation then it is used in reviews with similar scores and has high probability to be an opinion word.

$$Var(l) = \frac{\sum_{i=1}^{n} m_i^2 k_i}{k} - \left(\frac{\sum_{i=1}^{n} m_i k_i}{k}\right)^2$$

$$\sum_{i=1}^{n} k_i = k$$

where l – considered lemma, n – total count of the reviews in the collection, m_i – i-th review score, k_i – frequency of the lemma in the i-th review (may be 0).

Frequency of words, which start with the capital letter. The meaning of this feature is the frequency (in the review corpus) of each word starting with the capital letter and not located at the beginning of the sentence. With this feature we are trying to identify potential proper names, which are always neutral.

3.4 Feature and Collection Combinations

For our experiments we took top ten thousand words ordered by frequency from the movie review collection.

For each word from this list we had the following combinations of features and collections:

- TFIDF calculation using the pairs of collections: *small-news*, *small-description*, *opinion-news*, *opinion-description*;
- Weirdness calculation using the pairs of collections: *opinion-news* and *opinion-description* with document count and *small-description*, *opinion-description* with frequency;
- Deviation from the average score;
- Word score variance
- Word frequency in *opinion* and *small collections*;
- Total number of documents in the *opinion corpus*, where the word occurs;
- Frequency of capitalized words.

In addition, separately for description corpus we calculated the following features: frequency, document count, weirdness using *description-news collections* with document count and TFIDF using the same pair. Thus, each term had 18 features.

3.5 Algorithms and Evaluation

To train supervised machine learning algorithms we needed a set of labeled opinion words. We decided to label the full list of ten thousand words manually and then to use cross-validation. We marked up word as opinion one in case we could imagine it in any opinion context in the movie domain. All words were tagged by two authors.

As a result of our mark up we obtained the list of 3200 opinion words (1262 adjectives, 296 adverbs, 857 nouns, 785 verbs).

Our aim in this part of work was to classify words into two classes: opinion or neutral.

For this purpose Weka[1] data mining tool was used. We considered the following algorithms: *Logistic Regression* and *LogitBoost*. For all experiments 10 fold cross-validation was used.

Using aforementioned algorithms we obtained term lists, ordered by the predicted probability of their opinion orientation. To measure the quality of these lists we used *Precision@n* metric. This metric is very convenient for measuring the quality of list combinations and it can be used with different thresholds. For the algorithms quality comparison in different domains we chose n = 1000. This level is not too large for manual labeling and demonstrates the quality in an appropriate way.

The results of classification are in Table 1.

Logistic Regression	LogitBoost	Sum
66.00%	66.80%	70.90%

Table 1. *Precision@1000* of word classification

We noticed that the lists of opinion words extracted using two logistic algorithms differ significantly. So we decided to sum the weights of words in these two lists. The result of this summation can be found in the last column of the Table 1 and on the Figure 1.

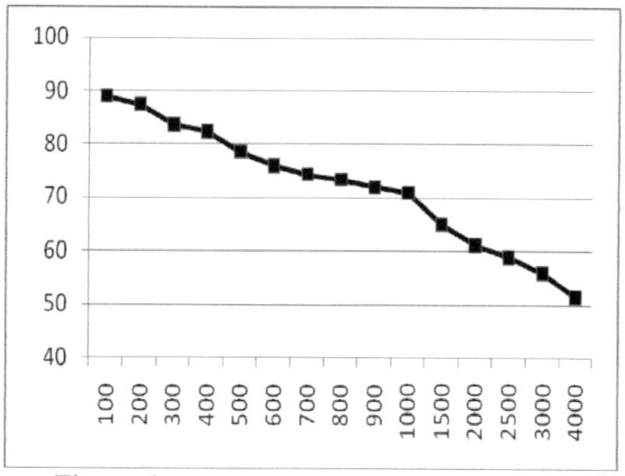

Figure 1. *Precision@n* in the Sum list (depending on n)

As the baseline for our experiments we used lists ordered by frequency in the review collection and Deviation from the average score. *Precision@1000* in these lists was 27.5% and 40.5% accordingly. Thus our algorithms gave significant improvements over baseline. All the other features can be found in Table 2.

Let us look at some examples of opinion words with the high probability value in the sum list:

Trogatel'nyi (affective), otstoi (trash), fignia (crap), otvratitel'no (disgustingly), posredstvenniy (satisfactory), predskazuemyi (predictable), ljubimyj (love) etc.

Obtained opinion word lists can be utilized in various sentiment analysis tasks. For example

[1] http://www.cs.waikato.ac.nz/ml/weka/

words can be used as features for document classification by the overall sentiment.

Feature	Collection	Precision @1000
TFIDF	small – news	39.2%
TFIDF	small – descr	36.3%
TFIDF	review – news	33.8%
TFIDF	review – descr	30.4%
Weirdness	review – news (doc. count)	51.1%
Weirdness	review – descr (doc. count)	47.7%
Weirdness	small – descr (frequency)	49.2%
Weirdness	review – descr (frequency)	46.0%
Deviation from the average score	review	40.5%
Word score variance	review	31.7%
Frequency	review	27.5%
Frequency	small	32.1%
Document Count	review	27.9%

Table 2. *Precision@1000* for different features

In [Chetviorkin et. al, 2011] we used opinion words in three-way review classification task and improved the quality of classification using opinion word weights.

3.6 Collection and Feature Selection

Finally, we studied the impact of each collection to the resulting quality of the opinion word classification. All collections (except review collection) were consequently excluded from constructing features. Additionally influence of the deviation from the average score, word score variance and frequency of words starting with capital letter were explored. In Table 3 results of classification with different feature sets can be found.

Thus, one can see that all collections and features improve the quality of classification. Exclusion of the description collection yields practically identical results for the sum list. Nevertheless this collection is very useful from model utilization in other domains (without it quality drops significantly).

Feature	Logistic Regression	Logit-Boost	Sum
All \ small collection	60.7%	66.7%	66.5%
All \ descr collection	61.3%	67.2%	70.6%
All \ news collection	66.1%	67.1%	69.0%
All \ deviation from the average score	64.4%	64.1%	68.6%
All \ word score variance	62.9%	64.3%	67.6%
All \ frequency of capitalized words	61.1%	61.7%	64.4%

Table 3. *Precision@1000* for different feature sets

4 Model Utilization to Similar Domains

In the previous section we constructed a new model for domain-specific opinion word extraction. We want to utilize this model in the other domains and evaluate the quality of obtained word lexicons and their combinations.

4.1 Data

We collected data on two more domains: book domain and computer games domain. The structure of the data was the same as for movie domain. Book and games review collections contained 16497 book reviews and 7928 game reviews of various genres accordingly. For each review, user's score on a ten-point scale was extracted.

The contrast collections of texts for book domain and games domain contained 24555 book descriptions and 1853 game descriptions.

Here we used the same **news corpus** as for movie domain.

4.2 Model Utilization and Evaluation

For new domains we extracted ten thousand the most frequent words (or all available words with frequency more then 3) and calculated all statistical features, which were described in Section 3.3. At the next step we applied our model trained in the movie domain to the book and games word lists. To evaluate the quality of word classification in new domains we manually labeled first thousand of words in each list. The results of classification are in Table 4.

	Logistic Regression	LogitBoost	Sum
Books	69.60%	59.10%	72.20%
Games	49.40%	63.00%	62.90%

Table 4. Results of the classification in book and games domains.

At the final step we took linear combination of the words (sum of word weights) in each list from three different domains (6 lists). The *Precision@1000* of the obtained opinion word list was **82.0%.**

We supposed that this general opinion word lexicon could improve the quality of the best list obtained in the movie domain. We summed weights of the best combined list in movie domain and general one (from three domain lists). Weights of the latter list were normalized previously. The quality of obtained movie domain-specific word dictionary was **71.8%. So exploitation of opinion words from other similar domains improved extraction of opinion words in the initial domain (+1.26%).**

5 Conclusion

In this paper, we described a method for opinion word extraction for any domain on the basis of several domain specific text collections. We utilized our algorithm in different domains and showed that it had good generalization abilities. The quality of the combined list was significantly better then the quality of each single list. Usage of the combined list improved extraction of opinion words in the initial domain.

Acknowledgements. This work is partially supported by RFBR grant N11-07-00588-a.

References

Ahmad K., Gillam L., Tostevin L. 1999. *University of Surrey participation in Trec8: Weirdness indexing for logical documents extrapolation and retrieval* In the Proceedings of Eigth Text Retrieval Conference (Trec-8).

Callan J.P., Croft W.B., Harding S.M. 1992. *The INQUERY Retrieval System* Proc. of Database and Expert System Applications DEXA-92, 3rd International Conference on Database and Expert Systems Applications / A.M. Tjoa and I. Ramos (eds.). – Springer Verlag, New York, pp.78-93.

Chetviorkin I. and Loukachevitch N. 2011. *Three-way movie review classification.* In International Conference on Computational Linguistics Dialog.

Choi Y. and Cardie C. 2009 *Adapting a polarity lexicon using integer linear programming for domain-specific sentiment classification.* In EMNLP '09, pages 590–598.

Ding X., Liu B., and Yu P. S. 2008. *A holistic lexicon-based approach to opinion mining*. In WSDM '08, pages 231–240.

Esuli A., Sebastiani F. 2005 *Determining the Semantic Orientation of Terms through Gloss Classification.* In: Conference of Information and Knowledge Management

Hu M., Liu B. 2004. *Mining and Summarizing Customer Reviews.* KDD

Jijkoun V., de Rijke M., and Weerkamp W. 2010. *Generating focused topic-specific sentiment lexicons.* In ACL '10, pages 585–594,

Kanayama H. and Nasukawa T. 2006. *Fully automatic lexicon expansion for domain-oriented sentiment analysis.* In EMNLP '06, pages 355–363, Morristown, NJ, USA.

Lu Y., Castellanos M., Dayal U. and Zhai C. 2011. *Automatic Construction of a Context-Aware Sentiment Lexicon: An Optimization Approach* In Proceedings of the World Wide Web Conference (WWW)

Neviarouskaya A., Prendinger H., and Ishizuka M. 2009. *Sentiful: Generating a reliable lexicon for sentiment analysis.* In ACII, pages 1–6, sep. 2009.

Pan, S. J., Ni, X., Sun, J-T, Yang, Q. and Chen, Z. 2010. *Cross-Domain Sentiment Classification via Spectral Feature Alignment.* In Proceedings of the World Wide Web Conference (WWW)

Pang B., Lee L. 2008. *Opinion mining and sentiment analysis. Foundations and Trends® in Information Retrieval.* Now Publishers

Turney P.D. 2002. *Thumbs Up or Thumbs Down? Semantic Orientation Applied to Unsupervised Classification of Reviews.* In: Proceedings of ACL. pp. 417-424.

The Role of Predicates in Opinion Holder Extraction

Michael Wiegand and **Dietrich Klakow**
Spoken Language Systems
Saarland University
D-66123 Saarbrücken, Germany
{Michael.Wiegand|Dietrich.Klakow}@lsv.uni-saarland.de

Abstract

In this paper, we investigate the role of predicates in opinion holder extraction. We will examine the shape of these predicates, investigate what relationship they bear towards opinion holders, determine what resources are potentially useful for acquiring them, and point out limitations of an opinion holder extraction system based on these predicates. For this study, we will carry out an evaluation on a corpus annotated with opinion holders. Our insights are, in particular, important for situations in which no labeled training data are available and only rule-based methods can be applied.

1 Introduction

One of the most important tasks in sentiment analysis is opinion holder extraction in which the entities uttering an opinion, also known as *opinion holders*, need to be extracted from a natural language text. For example, the opinion holders in (1) and (2) are *the vet* and *Russia*, respectively.

1. The owner put down the animal, although the vet had **forbidden** him to do so.
2. Russia **favors** creation of "international instruments" to regulate emissions.

As this is an entity extraction problem it can be considered as a typical task in information extraction. Though there is much work on that subject, most work focuses on data-driven methods. Thus, to a great extent it fails to fully describe certain linguistic aspects of that task.

In this work, we will have a close look at the role of predicates involved in opinion holder extraction. Predictive predicates for this task are, for example, *forbidden* in (1) and *favors* in (2). Unlike previous work, we will examine predicates in isolation. This means we do not consider them as some feature used in a data-driven classifier but as a part of an unsupervised rule-based extraction system which almost exclusively relies on them.

Apart from carrying out a quantitative examination regarding the shape of these predicates and the relationship they bear towards opinion holders, our main contributions of this paper are the investigation of what lexical resources are potentially useful for acquiring predictive predicates and pointing out the limitations of opinion holder extraction based on these predicates.

Our insights are important for building opinion holder extraction systems, in particular, rule-based systems. In particular, we hope that our analysis will provide a realistic rule-based baseline for opinion holder extraction. We also believe that many observations from this paper carry over to languages other than English. For only few of them, there are some corpora annotated with opinion holder information available. For all the remaining languages, rule-based systems leveraging the insights of this paper could be an option for automatic analysis.

2 Related Work

There has been much research on supervised learning for opinion holder extraction. Choi et al. (2005) examine opinion holder extraction using CRFs with several manually defined linguistic features and automatically learnt surface patterns. Bethard et al. (2004) and Kim and Hovy (2006) explore the usefulness of semantic roles provided by FrameNet (Fillmore et al., 2003) for both opinion holder and opinion target extraction. The approaches of those two papers have mostly been evaluated on some artificial data sets. More recently, Wiegand and Klakow (2010) explored convolution kernels for opinion holder extraction.

Rule-based opinion holder extraction heavily relies on lexical cues. Bloom et al. (2007) use a list of manually compiled communication verbs and

Proceedings of the Workshop on Information Extraction and Knowledge Acquisition, pages 13–20,
Hissar, Bulgaria, 16 September 2011.

identify opinion holders as noun phrases having a specific grammatical relation towards those verbs. The rule-based classifiers we evaluate in this work stem from this basic idea. However, we extend this classifier, for example, by considering a more diverse set of predicates and different grammatical relations.

Another work closely related to this study is (Ruppenhofer et al., 2008) which presents a roadmap to both opinion holder and target extraction outlining diverse linguistic phenomena involved in these tasks. In this work, we focus on the role of predicates. Moreover, we also carry out a quantitative evaluation of those related phenomena. Unlike Ruppenhofer et al. (2008), we thus try to identify the most immediate problems of this task. By also considering resources in order to solve these problems we hope to be a helpful guide for practitioners building an opinion holder extraction system from scratch.

3 Data

As a labeled (test) corpus, we use the MPQA 2.0 corpus[1] which is a large text corpus containing fine-grained sentiment annotation. It (mainly) consists of news texts which can be considered as a primary domain for opinion holder extraction. Other popular domains for sentiment analysis, for example, product reviews contain much fewer opinion holders according to the pertaining data sets (Kessler et al., 2010; Toprak et al., 2010). Opinions uttered in those texts usually express the author's point of view. Therefore, the extraction of sources of opinions is of minor importance.

We use the definition of opinion holders as described in (Wiegand and Klakow, 2010), i.e. every source of a *private state* or a *subjective speech event* (Wiebe et al., 2003) is considered an opinion holder. This is a very strict definition and the scores produced in this work can only be put into relation to the numbers presented in (Wiegand and Klakow, 2010). The final corpus comprises approximately 11,000 sentences with more than 6,200 opinion holders.

4 Examination of Predicates

4.1 The Different Types of Predicates

Table 1 displays the distribution of the different predicate types. We divided them into three categories being: unigram predicates (*verb*[2], *noun* and *adj*), multiword expressions of common syntactic structures (i.e. *verb+object*, *verb+prepObject*, *have+object* and *phrasal verb*) and a category for everything else. The table shows that the unigram predicates are most frequent. Since they cover almost 90% of the opinion holder predicate instances, we will focus on these expressions in the following experiments.

4.2 The Different Types of Grammatical Relations

Table 2 shows the distribution of the most frequent grammatical relations between opinion holder and its related predicate listed separately for each unigram predicate type. We use the Stanford parser (Klein and Manning, 2003) for obtaining all syntactic information. The table displays the percentage of that grammatical relation *within* the particular predicate type when it is observed as a predicate of an opinion holder in our labeled data set (*Perc.*)[3], the property of being a fairly reliable relation for a semantic *agent* (*Agent*), and the precision of that grammatical relation in conjunction with that opinion holder predicate type for detecting opinion holders (*Precision*). As a gold-standard of opinion holder predicates we extracted all unigram predicates from our data set that co-occur at least twice with an actual opinion holder.[4]

One may wonder why we did not mark the relation *nsubj* for nouns as *Agent* while the relation is marked as such for the other parts of speech. We found that subjects of predicate nouns can very often be found in constructions like (3). Clearly, *this* is not an agent of *idea*.

3. This is really an unwise **idea**. *[nsubj(This,idea)]*

Table 2 shows that there are some specific grammatical relations that co-occur frequently with opinion holders. These relations are exactly those implying an agent. Moreover, these relations are also the ones with the highest precision.

This insight may suggest using semantic-role labeling (SRL) for this task. We deliberately stick to using syntactic parsing since most publicly available SRL-systems only consider verb

[1] www.cs.pitt.edu/mpqa/databaserelease

[2] Note that by *verb*, we always only refer to full verbs, i.e. auxiliary and modal verbs are excluded.

[3] Note that for verbs we display relations with a lower percentage (>1%) than for nouns or adjectives (>4%) since verb predicates occur much more often.

[4] Singletons may be fairly noisy which is why we omit them.

Predicate Type	Frequency	Percentage	Example
verb	4272	70.89	I **believe** that this is more than that.
noun	948	15.73	This includes a growing **reluctance** by foreign companies to invest in the region.
adj	201	3.34	Ordinary Venezuelans are even less **happy** with the local oligarchic elite.
verb+object	234	3.88	Some officials **voiced concern** that China could secure concessions on Taiwan.
verb+prepObject	58	0.96	The United States **stands on** the Israeli **side** in dealing with the Middle East situation.
have+object	40	0.66	The KMM **had** no **confidence** in the democratic system.
phrasal verb	34	0.56	Washington **turned down** that protocol six months ago.
else	239	3.97	*NA*

Table 1: Distribution of the different opinion predicates.

Type	Relation	Perc.	Agent	Precision	Example
verb	↓nsubj	80.59	✓	47.47	China had always firmly **opposed** the US Taiwan Affairs Act.
verb	↓by_obj	2.69	✓	29.89	The agreements signed in 1960 for Cyprus were **considered** as nonexistent by many countries.
verb	↑rcmod	2.55		10.03	It was the President who **banned** postal voting by all Zimbabweans outside their constituencies.
verb	↓nsubjpass	1.50		8.85	I am **shocked**.
verb	↓dobj	1.24		2.38	Washington **angered** Beijing last year.
verb	↑partmod	1.08		7.13	Mugabe has no moral excuse for shooting people **demanding** a new constitution.
noun	↓poss	45.04	✓	44.56	President Bush's **declaration** touched off questions around the globe.
noun	↓of_obj	10.75		19.06	Through the **protests** of local labor groups, foreign laborers' working rights were protected.
noun	↓nsubj	6.12		6.42	Chavez is a staunch **supporter** of oil production cuts.
adj	↓nsubj	75.12	✓	71.63	We are **grateful** for the strong support expressed by the international community.
adj	↑amod	4.98		6.48	Soldiers **loyal** to the sacked chief of army staff exchanged gunfire with presidential guard units.

Table 2: Distribution of the different grammatical relations (percentage measured within predicate type).

predicates. Given our statistical analysis in Table 1, however, we would exclude a large portion of predicates, i.e. nouns and adjectives, if we used the output of a standard SRL-system.

It is interesting to note that there are also verbs occurring in argument positions that are definitely not agentive, i.e. *↓dobj* and *↓nsubjpass*. We inspected these cases in order to find out whether there is a set of verbs that systematically realizes opinion holders in non-agentive positions. Table 3 lists those verbs we found in our data set. 87.5% of them are also part of the so-called *amuse verbs*, a subset of transitive *psych-verbs* whose object is an experiencer and their subject is the cause of the psychological state (Levin, 1993). The subject, i.e. the cause (this does not even have to be a person), is unlikely to be the opinion holder, whereas the experiencer is often observed to denote such an entity.

4.3 The Different Resources for Opinion Holder Predicates

In this section, we want to examine in how far existing resources contain predicates that usually co-occur with opinion holders. The resources we consider are different in their design and serve diverse purposes. Only one has been specifically designed for opinion holder extraction. For the remaining resources, there may be some modification necessary, for example, by selecting a subset. As we want to examine these resources for an unsupervised (open-domain) rule-based method, these modifications should be pretty simple, fast to implement, and not require extensive knowledge about our particular data set.

4.3.1 Communication Verbs from Appraisal Lexicon (AL)

The communication verbs from Appraisal Lexicon (*AL*) are the only lexicon that has been designed for opinion holder extraction (Bloom et al., 2007). With 260 entries, it is the smallest resource in this paper. Little is known about the creation of this resource (e.g. whether the resource has been optimized for some domain) except that several verb classes from Levin (1993) have been considered.

alienate	concern	exasperate	lure	rile
anger	cow	frighten	obsess	scare
annoy	disappoint	frustrate	offend	shock
astonish	discourage	humiliate	persuade	stunt
baffle	disgust	infuriate	please	suit
bias	disturb	intimidate	rankle	surprise
bother	embarrass	irk	relieve	tear
captivate	enrage	irritate	remind	worry

Table 3: Predicates taking opinion holders in a non-agentive argument position.

appoint	conjecture	admire	correspond	say
characterize	see	marvel	assessment	want
dub	sight	complain	transfer of message	long
declare	judgment	advise	manner of speaking	tell

Table 4: Levin's verb classes taking opinion holders in agentive argument position (only *amuse verbs* take opinion holder in non-agentive positions).

4.3.2 Subjectivity Lexicon (SL)

The Subjectivity Lexicon (*SL*) from the MPQA-project (Wilson et al., 2005) is one of the most commonly used sentiment lexicons. The lexicon contains 8222 subjective expressions from different parts of speech. For our experiments we will only consider its verbs, nouns and adjectives.

This lexicon has been used for various subtasks in sentiment analysis, primarily subjectivity detection and polarity classification (Wilson et al., 2005). It has also been used for opinion holder extraction (Choi et al., 2005; Wiegand and Klakow, 2010) though the lexicon does not contain any annotation specifically designed for this task which is why each entry is considered *some clue* for an opinion in a sentence. In this work, we will even assume each entry to be a predicate predictive for opinion holder extraction.

Since this resource is fairly large, we also consider the subset SL_{strong} consisting of (fairly unambiguous) *strong-subjective* expressions.

4.3.3 Levin's Verb Classes (Levin)

Even though *AL* already considers verb classes from Levin (1993), we constructed a separate subset from that resource for this study. The reason for this is that we found that there are many relevant verbs (e.g. *agree*, *deem* or *disapprove*) not contained in *AL* but that are part of Levin's lexicon. Our selection method was ad-hoc but we did not tune this resource for any particular data set, i.e we included every verb class in our lexicon of which the majority were verbs we would associate *a priori* with opinion holders.

Another important aspect of Levin's work (as already mentioned in §4.2) is that it allows a distinction of verbs taking opinion holders in agentive argument positions and verbs taking them in other positions. We identified *amuse verbs* to be precisely the latter class. (Note that *AL* completely excludes this class.) Admittedly, other resources, such as FrameNet, also encode that distinction. Unfortunately, using FrameNet for an unsupervised classifier would be more difficult. We would need to choose from 1049 (partially overlapping) frames.[5] In Levin's lexicon, we only needed to choose from 193 classes. The final selection is shown in Table 4.

4.3.4 WordNet - Lexicographer files (WN-LF)

WordNet[6] is possibly the largest and most popular general-purpose lexico-semantic ontology for the English language. Most work using this resource focuses on the relationship between the different synsets, i.e. the groups of synonymous words that represent the nodes in the ontology graph. Due to the high number of these synsets, we found it very difficult to select an appropriate subset predictive for opinion holder extraction. This is why we tried to harness another form of word grouping that this resource provides. The *lexicographer files* (*WN-LF*) seem to operate on a more suitable level of granularity. The entire ontology (i.e. the set of synsets) is divided in 44 of such *files* where each file represents a very general semantic word class (e.g. *noun.food* or *verb.motion*). We consider the files *noun.cognition*, *noun.communication*, *verb.cognition* and *verb.communication*. Due to the coarse-grained nature of the *WN-LF*, the resulting set of words contains 10151 words (7684 nouns and 2467 verbs).

Table 5 summarizes the properties of the different resources. Due to the high number of nouns in *WN-LF*, we will evaluate this lexicon both with and without nouns. For all resources only containing verbs, we also use Nomlex (Macleod et al., 1998) to find corresponding noun predicates, e.g.

[5] according to: `http://framenet.icsi.berkeley.edu/`

[6] `wordnet.princeton.edu`

Resource	Abbrev.	Size	Parts of Speech	Description
Subjectivity Lexicon	SL	8222	verbs, nouns and adjs	resource built for sentiment analysis in general
Subjectivity Lexicon - strong	SL_{strong}	5569	verbs, nouns and adjs	subset of SL with exprs. having a strong subjective connotation
Communication Verbs	AL	260 (354)	verbs	resource built for opinion holder extraction
Levin's Verb Classes	Levin	715 (869)	verbs	general purpose resource
WordNet Lexicographer Files	WN-LF	10151	verbs and nouns	general purpose resource
		2467 (2948)	only verbs (from WN)	

Table 5: Properties of the different resources (numbers in brackets denote the size of a resource including nouns obtained by Nomlex extension).

believe (verb) → *belief* (noun), as we already established in Table 1 that nouns play a significant part in the recognition of opinion holders.

4.4 Comparison of Resources

Table 6 displays the performance of the different resources when used in a simple rule-based opinion holder classifier. It classifies a noun phrase (NP) as an opinion holder when the NP is an agent (according to the unambiguous grammatical relations from Table 2)[7] of an entry in a particular lexicon. Only for the *amuse verbs* in *Levin*, we consider the other grammatical relations ↓*nsubjpass* and ↓*dobj*.

The different resources produce quite different results. Surprisingly, *SL* is the lowest performing resource even though it has been used in previous work (Choi et al., 2005; Wiegand and Klakow, 2010). Though the recall increases by adding nouns and adjectives to verbs, the precision notably drops. For the subset SL_{strong} the precision drops slightly less so that the F-Score always increases when the other parts of speech are added to the verbs. Overall, SL_{strong} has a much higher precision than *SL* and its F-Score (considering all parts of speech) is on a par with *SL* even though it is a significantly smaller word list (see Table 5). *SL* is a resource primarily built for subjectivity and polarity classification and these results suggest that the lexical items to imply opinion holders are only partially overlapping with those clues.

Though *AL* and *Levin* are considerably smaller than *SL*, they perform better. Moreover, *Levin* is considerably better than *AL*. In both cases, the extension by noun predicates using Nomlex results in a marginal yet consistent improvement. Unfortunately, the usage of the *amuse verbs* does not produce a notable improvement. We mostly ascribe it to the fact that those verbs occurred only

[7]By that we mean those relations marked with *Agent*.

Resource	Subtype	Prec	Rec	F1
SL	verb	42.25	27.54	33.34
	verb+noun	38.20	32.20	34.94
	verb+noun+adj	34.30	35.39	34.84
SL_{strong}	verb	**59.80**	20.17	30.17
	verb+noun	56.01	22.92	32.53
	verb+noun+adj	52.71	25.19	34.09
AL	plain	41.88	32.65	36.69
	+Nomlex	41.66	34.32	37.64
Levin	noAmuse	42.59	44.59	43.57
	withAmuse	42.12	45.74	43.86
	withAmuse+Nomlex	41.51	47.74	44.41
WN-LF	verb	33.49	65.44	44.31
	verb+noun	30.19	**71.33**	42.42
	verb+Nomlex	32.97	68.73	**44.56**

Table 6: Performance of the different resources on opinion holder extraction.

very infrequently (i.e. either once or twice in the entire data set).

WN-LF performs slightly better than *Levin*. Adding the large set of nouns is not effective. The set of verbs augmented by corresponding noun predicates obtained by Nomlex produces better results. The large F-Score of *WN-LF* is only due to a high recall. The precision is comparably low. For this task, another set of predicates maintaining a higher precision is clearly preferable.

4.5 Combination of the Resources

In this section, we combine the different resources (by that we mean taking the union of different resources). For each resource, we use the best performing configuration from the previous evaluation. Table 7 shows the performance of different combinations. As testing all combinations would be beyond the scope of this work, we mainly focus on combinations not using *WN-LF*.

Resource(s)	Prec	Rec	F1
WN-LF *(baseline)*	32.97	68.73	44.56
SL+AL	37.52	52.80	43.68
SL_{strong}+AL	**42.91**	49.69	46.05
SL+Levin	34.56	62.95	44.62
SL_{strong}+Levin	40.97	57.43	**47.82**
AL+Levin	41.49	47.80	44.42
SL+AL+Levin	34.56	62.95	44.62
SL_{strong}+AL+Levin	40.96	57.43	47.82
SL+AL+Levin+WN-LF	29.47	**78.28**	42.82
SL_{strong}+AL+Levin+WN-LF	32.19	75.32	45.10
OraclePRED	46.44	67.83	55.13
OraclePRED*	47.04	68.62	55.82

Table 7: Performance of combined resources.

We seek a classifier with a higher precision than that achieved by *WN-LF*. Combining *WN-LF* with other resources would only result in another increase in recall.

We also want to have an estimate of an upper bound of this method. *OraclePRED* uses all predicates that occur as a predicate of an opinion holder on our test set at least twice. We only consider predicates which have been observed in prototypical agentive positions. *OraclePRED** also uses the knowledge of the predicates from the data set but is not restricted to agentive patterns. That is, we store for each predicate the grammatical relation(s) with which it has been observed (e.g. *oppose+↓nsubj* or *anger+↓dobj*); we only consider the frequent grammatical relationships from Table 2. Thus, like semantic role labeling, we should be more flexible than a classifier that exclusively considers opinion holders to be in an agentive argument position of some predicate.

Table 7 shows that a combination of resources is indeed beneficial. SL_{strong} and *Levin* produce a higher F-Score than *WN-LF* by preserving a considerably higher precision. Adding *AL* to this set has no effect on performance, since the few predicates of *AL* are already in the union of SL_{strong}*+Levin*. Comparing the performance of the different configurations with *OraclePRED*, we can conclude that the resources that are considered are not exactly modeling opinion holder predicates but a combination of them does it to a large extent. Looking at the false negatives that the best configuration produced (note that we will discuss the issue of false positives in §4.6), we could not really make out a particular group of verbs that this classifier systematically excluded. As far as *Levin* is concerned, however, we assume that the fact that this typology only considers 3000 verbs *in total* also means that many infrequent verbs, such as *ratify* or *lobby*, have simply been excluded from consideration even though their behavior would enable an assignment to one of the existing verb classes.

The performance of *OraclePRED* also shows that opinion holder extraction is a really difficult task as this upper bound is fairly low in absolute numbers. The oracle using the grammatical relations (*OraclePRED**) improves performance only slightly. This is consistent with our experiments using *amuse verbs*.

4.6 Ambiguity of Predicates

In this section we evaluate individual predicates that occur very frequently and also state in which resources these expressions can be found. Table 8 shows that these predicates behave quite differently. The verb *say* is by far the most predictive individual predicate though this is mainly due to its high recall. Other verbs, such as *want*, *believe* or *think*, have a considerably lower recall but their precision is almost twice as high. In terms of coverage, *WN-LF* is the only resource that contains all expressions. This is consistent with its high recall that was measured in previous experiments. On the other hand, $SL_{(strong)}$ only contains a subset of these expressions but the expressions are mostly those with a very high precision.

The individual examination of highly frequent predicates shows that a problem inherent in opinion holder extraction based on predicates is the lacking precision of predicates. In general, we do not think that the false positives produced by our best configuration are due to the fact that there are many predicates on the list which are wrong in general. Omitting a verb with a low precision, such as *say* or *call*, is not an option as it would always heavily degrade recall.

5 Other Clues for Opinion Holder Extraction

In this section, we want to put opinion holder predicates into relation to other clues for opinion holder extraction. We consider two types of clues that can be automatically computed. Both aim at improving precision when added to the clue based on opinion holder predicates since this clue

Pred	In Resources	Prec	Rec	F1
say	AL,Levin,WN-LF	42.52	**13.62**	**20.64**
want	Levin,$SL_{(strong)}$,WN-LF	**83.12**	2.04	3.99
call	Levin,WN-LF	53.66	1.41	2.74
believe	AL,Levin,$SL_{(strong)}$,WN-LF	79.46	1.42	2.79
support	AL,Levin,SL,WN-LF	71.08	0.94	1.86
think	AL,Levin,$SL_{(strong)}$,WN-LF	79.78	1.13	2.24
tell	Levin,WN-LF	35.68	1.21	2.35
know	AL,Levin,$SL_{(strong)}$,WN-LF	66.33	1.04	2.04
agree	Levin,$SL_{(strong)}$,WN-LF	63.64	0.89	1.76
decide	SL,WN-LF	69.81	0.59	1.17

Table 8: Individual performance of the 10 most frequent opinion holder predicates.

already provides a comparatively high recall.

The clue *PERSON* checks whether the candidate opinion holder is a person. For some ambiguous predicates, such as *critical*, this would allow a correct disambiguation, i.e. *Dr. Ren* in (4) would be classified as an opinion holder while *the cross-strait balance of military power* in (5) would not.

4. Dr. Ren was **critical** of the government's decision.

5. In his view, the cross-strait balance of military power is **critical** to the ROC's national security.

For this clue, we employ Stanford named-entity recognizer (Finkel et al., 2005) for detecting proper nouns and WordNet for recognizing common nouns denoting persons.

The second clue *SUBJ* detects subjective evidence in a sentence. The heuristics applied should filter false positives, such as (6).

6. "We do not have special devices for inspecting large automobiles and cargoes", Nazarov **said**.

If an opinion holder has been found according to our standard procedure using opinion holder predicates, some additional property must hold so that the classifier predicts an opinion holder. Either the candidate opinion holder phrase contains a subjective expression (7), some subjective expression modifies the predicate (8), or the proposition that is introduced by the opinion holder predicate[8] contains at least one subjective expression (9).

7. $Angry_{Subj}$ residents **looked** to Tsvangirai to confront the government.

8. Thousands **waited** $angrily_{Subj}$ to cast their votes.

9. Mr. Mugabe's associates **said** [it was a "bad_{Subj} decision"]$_{proposition}$.

[8] We identify these propositions as the yield of an SBAR complement of the opinion holder predicate.

The subjective expressions are again obtained by using the Subjectivity Lexicon (Wilson et al., 2005). Since in our previous experiments the subset of strong subjective expressions turned out to be effective, we examine another clue $SUBJ_{strong}$ which just focuses on this subset.

As we assume this kind of subjectivity detection to be very error prone, we also want to consider a related upper bound. This upper bound *allSPEECH* addresses the most frequently found reason for misclassifying an opinion holder on the basis of predicates, namely failing to distinguish between the underlying *objective* and *subjective* speech events. (We will focus on only this error source in this work, since the other error sources are much more infrequent and diverse. Their discussion would be beyond the scope of this paper.) We previously measured a fairly low precision of predicates denoting speech events, such as *say* or *tell*. This is due to the fact that these predicates may not only be involved in subjective speech events, such as (9), but may also introduce objective speech events, such as (6), that typically involve no opinion holder. Our upper bound *allSPEECH* undoes the distinction between different speech events in the gold standard (i.e. it always considers a source of a speech event as an opinion holder). Thus, we simulate how opinion holder extraction would work if this distinction could be perfectly automatically achieved.

Table 9 displays the results of various combinations. For the opinion holder predicates, we consider the best combination of resources from our previous experiments in §4.5 (*PRED*) and the upper bound of predicates (*OraclePRED**). The table shows that adding *PERSON* to *PRED* results in an improved F-Score. The addition of *SUBJ* increases precision while recall drops. *allSPEECH*, on the other hand, causes a boost in performance. Even though the combination of the two upper bounds *OraclePRED** and *allSPEECH* together with the *PERSON* filter would largely increase performance, the total F-Score of 65% shows that it would not completely solve this task.

6 Discussion

If we compare our best fully automatic result, i.e. *PRED+PERSON* with 49.90% (Table 9) with that of data-driven methods using the same corpus and task definition, for example Wiegand and Klakow (2010), who obtain an F-Score of almost 63%, one

Clues	Prec	Rec	F1
PRED	40.97	**57.43**	47.82
PRED+PERSON	48.67	51.21	**49.90**
PRED+SUBJ	48.04	32.77	38.97
PRED+SUBJ$_{strong}$	48.89	23.32	31.58
PRED+PERSON+SUBJ	57.84	29.87	39.39
PRED+PERSON+SUBJ$_{strong}$	**60.13**	21.24	31.39
PRED+allSPEECH	53.79	58.33	55.97
PRED+PERSON+allSPEECH	64.00	53.27	58.14
OraclePRED*+allSPEECH	60.21	67.92	63.83
OraclePRED*+PERSON+allSPEECH	69.67	61.59	65.38

Table 9: Performance of opinion holder predicates in conjunction with other clues.

still notices a considerable gap. Of course, this particular data-driven method should be regarded as an upper bound since it uses a very large labeled training set (§3) and even incorporates some lexical resources for feature engineering we almost exclusively rely on in our rule-based classifier (i.e. AL and SL). This also shows that it is really hard to build a rule-based classifier for opinion holder extraction.

7 Conclusion

In this paper, we examined the importance of predicates from diverse resources for the extraction of opinion holders. We found that strong subjective expressions from the Subjectivity Lexicon combined with a subset of Levin's verb classes contain very predictive words. A classifier extracting noun phrases in an unambiguous agentive position of these predicates results in an opinion holder classifier with both reasonable recall and precision but our upper bound shows that there is still room for improvement. Opinion holders in non-agentive positions are so infrequent in our test set that their consideration is less critical. The classifier based on opinion holder predicates can only be improved by restricting holder candidates to persons. Further filters ensuring subjectivity are too restrictive and thus cause a large decrease in recall. Our exploratory experiments show, however, that some additional improvement in opinion holder extraction could be achieved if subjective speech events could be better separated from objective ones.

Acknowledgements

This work was funded by the German Federal Ministry of Education and Research (Software-Cluster) under grant no. "01IC10S01" and the Cluster of Excellence for Multimodal Computing and Interaction. The authors would like to thank Josef Ruppenhofer for interesting discussions.

References

S. Bethard, H. Yu, A. Thornton, V. Hatzivassiloglou, and D. Jurafsky. 2004. Extracting Opinion Propositions and Opinion Holders using Syntactic and Lexical Cues. In *Computing Attitude and Affect in Text: Theory and Applications*.

K. Bloom, S. Stein, and S. Argamon. 2007. Appraisal Extraction for News Opinion Analysis at NTCIR-6. In *NTCIR-6*.

Y. Choi, C. Cardie, E. Riloff, and S. Patwardhan. 2005. Identifying Sources of Opinions with Conditional Random Fields and Extraction Patterns. In *HLT/EMNLP*.

C. J. Fillmore, C. R. Johnson, and M. R. Petruck. 2003. Background to FrameNet. *International Journal of Lexicography*, 16:235 – 250.

J. R. Finkel, T. Grenager, and C. Manning. 2005. Incorporating Non-local Information into Information Extraction Systems by Gibbs Sampling. In *ACL*.

J. Kessler, M. Eckert, L. Clarke, and N. Nicolov. 2010. The ICWSM JDPA 2010 Sentiment Corpus for the Automotive Domain. In *ICWSM-DCW*.

S. Kim and E. Hovy. 2006. Extracting Opinions, Opinion Holders, and Topics Expressed in Online News Media Text. In *ACL Workshop on Sentiment and Subjectivity in Text*.

D. Klein and C. D. Manning. 2003. Accurate Unlexicalized Parsing. In *ACL*.

B. Levin. 1993. *English Verb Classes and Alternations: A Preliminary Investigation*. University of Chicago Press.

C. Macleod, R. Grishman, A. Meyers, L. Barrett, and R. Reeves. 1998. NOMLEX: A Lexicon of Nominalizations. In *EURALEX*.

J. Ruppenhofer, S. Somasundaran, and J. Wiebe. 2008. Finding the Source and Targets of Subjective Expressions. In *LREC*.

C. Toprak, N. Jakob, and I. Gurevych. 2010. Sentence and Expression Level Annotation of Opinions in User-Generated Discourse. In *ACL*.

J. Wiebe, T. Wilson, and C. Cardie. 2003. Annotating Expressions of Opinions and Emotions in Language. *Language Resources and Evaluation*, 1:2.

M. Wiegand and D. Klakow. 2010. Convolution Kernels for Opinion Holder Extraction. In *HLT/NAACL*.

T. Wilson, J. Wiebe, and P. Hoffmann. 2005. Recognizing Contextual Polarity in Phrase-level Sentiment Analysis. In *HLT/EMNLP*.

Dependency-Based Text Compression for Semantic Relation Extraction

Marcos Garcia
Center for Research in
Information Technologies (CITIUS)
University of Santiago de Compostela
marcos.garcia.gonzalez@usc.es

Pablo Gamallo
Center for Research in
Information Technologies (CITIUS)
University of Santiago de Compostela
pablo.gamallo@usc.es

Abstract

The application of linguistic patterns and rules are one of the main approaches for Information Extraction as well as for high-quality ontology population. However, the lack of flexibility of the linguistic patterns often causes low coverage. This paper presents a weakly-supervised rule-based approach for Relation Extraction which performs partial dependency parsing in order to simplify the linguistic structure of a sentence. This simplification allows us to apply generic semantic extraction rules, obtained with a distant-supervision strategy which takes advantage of semi-structured resources. The rules are added to a partial dependency grammar, which is compiled into a parser capable of extracting instances of the desired relations. Experiments in different Spanish and Portuguese corpora show that this method maintains the high-precision values of rule-based approaches while improves the recall of these systems.

1 Introduction

In recent years, the interest in obtaining structured data from unstructured resources has been increased, namely due to the exponential growth of information in the Web. Regarding this objective, Relation Extraction (RE) aims to automatically identify semantic relations between entities. For instance, from the sentence "Nick Cave was born in the small town of Warracknabeal", a RE system may identify that Warracknabeal is the birthplace of Nick Cave.

The obtained data are arranged in machine-readable formats ("Nick Cave `hasBirthplace` Warracknabeal"), and then incorporated into databases and ontologies, used to improve applications such as Question Answering engines or Information Retrieval systems.

RE systems usually need a set of sentences containing instances of a semantic relation (e.g., `hasBirthplace`). These sentences are processed in order to provide a rich *linguistic space* with different knowledge (tokens, lemmas, PoS-tags, syntactic dependencies, etc.). This knowledge is used to extract semantic relations by (i) training machine-learning classifiers or by (ii) applying on large corpora lexico-syntactic patterns (LSP) derived from the linguistic space.

Relation Extraction approaches rely on the assumption that lexico-syntactic regularities (e.g., LSP) may characterize the same type of knowledge, such as semantic information. However, one of the main problems of these strategies is the low coverage of LSP, which varies with small differences in punctuation, adjective or adverb modification, etc. For instance, the previous example sentence could be represented in a great variety of manners:

- "Nick Cave was born in the small town of Warracknabeal"
- "Nick Cave was born in the town of Warracknabeal"
- "Nick Cave was born in Warracknabeal"
- "Nick Cave, born in the small town of Warracknabeal"

Both machine learning and pattern-matching approaches attempt to avoid this problem by using

Proceedings of the Workshop on Information Extraction and Knowledge Acquisition, pages 21–28,
Hissar, Bulgaria, 16 September 2011.

larger training data or by applying syntactic parsers that identify the constituents of a sentence as well as their functions. However, obtaining large collections of high-quality training data for different semantic relations is not always feasible, since a lot of manual effort is needed. Furthermore, parsers for other languages than English often perform very partial analyses, or are not freely available.

In this paper, we introduce a rule-based approach for RE that overcomes the low coverage problem by simplifying the linguistic structures: we perform a sort of sentence compression technique that uses partial dependency parsing to remove some satellite elements from the input of the extraction rules.

In order to obtain high-quality extraction rules, we use a distant-supervision strategy that takes advantage of semi-structures resources, such as Wikipedia infoboxes or Freebase:[1] First, large sets of semantically related pairs are used for automatically extracting and annotating sentences containing instances of the desired relation. Then, we transform these sentences into LSP, which are generalized through a longest common string algorithm. Finally, the generic patterns are converted into syntactico-semantic rules and added to a dependency grammar.

We performed several experiments with different semantic relations in Portuguese and Spanish, using encyclopedic and journalistic corpora. The results show that dependency-based text compression allows us to improve the recall without losing the high precision values of pattern-matching techniques.

This paper is organized as follows: Section 2 introduces some related work. Section 3 presents the motivation of our Relation Extraction method. Then, Sections 4 and 5 show the strategy for extracting patterns as well as the method for transforming them into semantic rules. In Section 6, some experiments are performed. Finally, Section 7 reports the conclusions of our work.

2 Related Work

In this section we briefly introduce some related work concerning text compression methods as well as strategies for semantic Relation Extraction.

In recent years, several approaches have been proposed for sentence compression, whose aim is to reduce the size of a text while preserving its essential information (Chandrasekar et al., 1996). There are statistical methods (with different degree of supervision) for sentence compression, which require training corpora in order to learn what constituents could be removed from the original input (Clarke and Lapata, 2006). Cohn and Lapata (2009) present Tree-to-Tree Transducer, a state-of-the-art sentence compression method which transforms a source parse tree into a compressed parse tree. We have to note that our approach differs from common sentence compression strategies in a key point: it is not centered in maintaining the grammaticality of a sentence, but just in simplifying its structure and keeping its essential information.

Regarding Relation Extraction, Hearst (1992) was the first one to experiment a pattern-based strategy for the identification of semantic relations, using a small set of initial patterns to get hyperonymy relations by means of a bootstrapping technique. In Brin (1998), a similar method is applied, but it only selects those patterns that show a good performance. Other works make use of Question-Answering pair examples to automatically extract patterns (Ravichandran and Hovy, 2002). A novelty of this system lies in the application of a suffix tree, leading to discover generalized patterns by calculating their common substrings.

In the previously cited work, the learning process starts with patterns that have high precision but low recall. So, recall is increased by automatically learning new patterns. By contrast, in Pantel and Pennacchiotti (2006), the starting point are patterns with high recall and low precision. The goal is to exploit these patterns by filtering incorrect related pairs using the Web. There are also interesting works using more supervised strategies for domain-specific corpora: in Aussenac-Gilles and Jacques (2006), it is described a method and a tool to manually define new specific patterns for specialized text corpora.

Recently, distant-supervision and self-supervised approaches take advantage of large amounts of freely available structured data, in order to automatically obtain training corpora to build extraction systems (Mintz et al., 2009; Hoffman et al., 2010).

Other works perform extraction in a different way. Open Information Extraction is a new paradigm that attempts to extract a large set of relational pairs with-

[1] `www.wikipedia.org` and `www.freebase.com`

out manually specifying semantic relations (Etzioni et al., 2008). *woe* is an Open Information Extraction method that takes advantage of the high quality semi-structures resources of Wikipedia (Wu and Weld, 2010). Finally, Bollegala's Relational Duality (Bollegala et al., 2010) applies a sequential co-clustering algorithm in order to cluster different LSP for extracting relations.

3 Motivation

The method presented in this paper follows a common statement which suggests that some linguistic constructs reliably convey the same type of knowledge, such as semantic or ontological relations (Aussenac-Gilles and Jacques, 2006; Aguado de Cea et al., 2009). Furthermore, it is based on the following assumption:

> *Semantic relations can be expressed in the same simple way as syntactic dependencies*

A semantic relation found in a sentence can be usually represented by a dependency link between two entities, even if there are items of extra information that can make the sentence very complex. This extra information does not express the target relation, but it may extend the meaning of the related entities or introduce knowledge not relevant for the relation. Among the most frequent patterns expressing relations, we can find variations of the same *original* pattern, which differ by the existence of modifiers, coordination, etc. Since these simple patterns have high precision, it is crucial to find a way of making them still more generic to increase coverage. For this purpose, we follow a two-step strategy:

1. Sentence compression: We use a partial grammar that establishes syntactic dependencies between items of extra information (modifiers, adjuncts, punctuation...). The grammar maintains only the dependency Heads and therefore allows us to obtain a sort of simplified linguistic structure.

2. Pattern extraction: We extract LSP, which are then simplified by means of a longest common string algorithm. These simplified patterns are transformed into generic semantic rules and added to our dependency grammar.

The combination of both standard dependency rules and generic semantic rules for RE allows the system to increase coverage without losing precision.

4 Partial Parsing for Sentence Compression

One of the main processes of our strategy attempts to simplify linguistic structures in order to easily extract their information. For this purpose, we use an open-source suite of multilingual syntactic analysis, DepPattern (Gamallo and González, 2011). The suite includes basic grammars for five languages as well as a compiler to build parsers from each one. The parser takes as input the output of a PoS-tagger, in our case, FreeLing (Padró et al., 2010), which also lemmatizes the sentences and performs Named Entity Recognition and Classification (NER/NEC).

The basic grammars of DepPattern contain rules for many types of linguistic phenomena, from noun modification to more complex structures such as apposition or coordination. However, for our simplification task, only some types of dependencies are required, in particular those that compress the sentences maintaining their basic meaning. Following other strategies for sentence compression (Molina et al., 2010), we modified the default grammar by making use of rules that identify the following satellites and subordinate constituents:

- Punctuation (quotation marks, commas, brackets, etc.).
- Common noun and adjective coordination.
- Noun, Adverb, and Adjectival Phrases.
- Prepositional complements, verbal periphrasis and apposition.
- Negative sentences (where the verb inherits the negative tag).

After running the parser, all the Dependents identified by these rules are removed. That is, we obtain a compressed structure without satellites, modifiers, etc. In 1 and 2 we can see two examples of our partial parsing. The elements at the tail of the arrows are the Dependents, while those at the front of the arrows are the Heads.

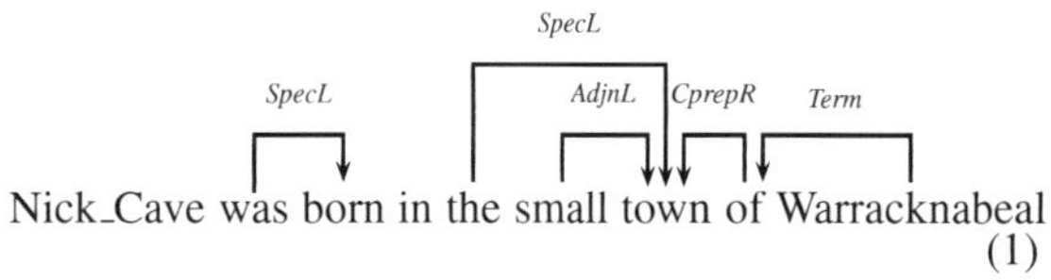

(1)

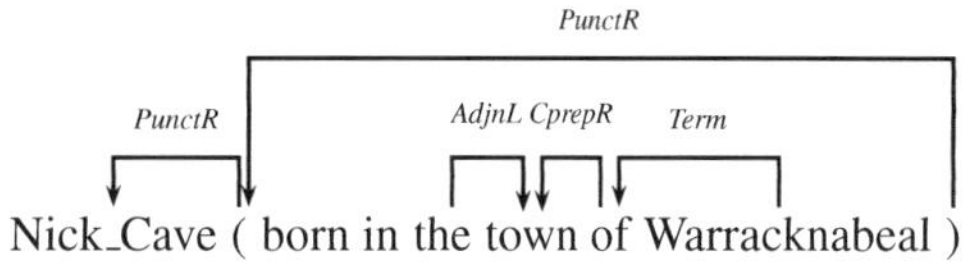

(2)

Taking into account that only the Heads (that are not Dependents) are maintained, the compression process on the two initial sentences will produce an unique simplified structure (note that the Heads of location phrases ("town of NP", "region of NP", etc.) inherit the location information provided by the dependent proper nouns, so in the examples, "town" represents a specific location):

<**Nick_Cave** *born in* **town**>

Generic semantic rules are then applied on these structures. For instance:

> if a personal name is the Head, a location noun is the Dependent, and the verb "to be born" is a Relator, then a `hasBirthplace` relation is identified.

This rule can be proposed to cover both the previous examples as well as many others. Moreover, our parsing also prevents from applying the previous extraction rule on sentences such as 3, where the Head of the first Noun Phrase is not the personal name, but a common noun ("son").

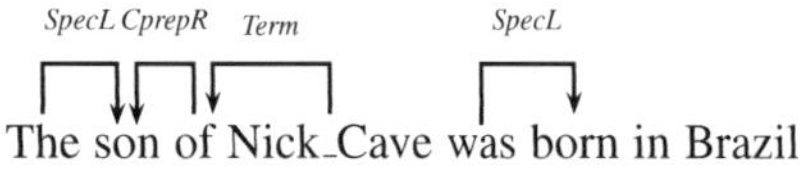

(3)

<**son** *born in* **Brazil**>

This way, in this type of sentences (or in negative ones, where the verb has a *negative* tag), our semantic rule will not extract the incorrect pair "Nick Cave `hasBirthplace` Brazil" (but we will be able to know the birthplace of "the son of Nick Cave").

The grammar formalism also allows the parser to maintain the Dependents of a rule after the rule application. Therefore, if we want to add several sets of rules for extracting various relations, the system will only need a single pass over the corpus.

In sum, the sentence compression performed by partial parsing simplifies the linguistic structures maintaining their basic information. This way, the addition of generic semantic rules (converted from LSP) at the end of a depedency grammar allows the parser to increase the coverage of the extraction.

5 Obtaining the Patterns and Rules

This section presents the distant-supervision method for extracting the lexico-syntactic patterns as well as the strategy for generating the generic rules.

5.1 Pattern Extraction

Following the assumption that most instances of a semantic relation are represented by similar LSP, we intend to obtain examples of those patterns and extract from them their *original* structures (without extra information), then transformed into semantic rules. In order to automate this process, we use the following strategy:

We get a large set of entity pairs of a desired relation from (semi)structured resources. For instance, for the `hasBirthplace` relation we get pairs from Wikipedia infoboxes (e.g., "Nick Cave - Warracknabeal", "Josep Guardiola - Sampedor", etc.). Note that the attributes of many relations are language-dependent (e.g., "Nick Cave" `hasProfession`: English: "singer/songwriter"; Spanish: "cantante/cantautor"; Portuguese: "cantor/cantautor", etc.), so the use of resources like Freebase is not always feasible. If we do not have a large amount of pairs, we manually introduce a small set of pairs regarding a particular relation.

These pairs are used to select from the unstructured text of Wikipedia sentences that contain both a named entity and an attribute of the relation. If the two terms match a known pair of the initial list, the example is annotated as positive. Otherwise, it is annotated as negative. Note that if we have a large set of pairs, the method does not require bootstrapping. However, If we only have a small set of initial pairs, a bootstrapping process is required (we use this strategy if the number of positive sentences is less than n, where n was empirically set to 200). Then, each selected sentence is tokenized, lemma-

Sentence: Nick Cave was born in the town of Warracknabeal.

Polarity: **Nick Cave** `hasBirthplace` **Warracknabeal**, true.

Pattern: <**X** be_V born_V in_PRP DA town_N of_PRP **Y**>

Figure 1: Example of a Sentence with the Polarity label of the related terms and its Pattern (V means verb, DT determiner, PRP preposition and N common noun).

tized and PoS-tagged. We also apply a NEC, in order to semantically classify the named entities.

Finally, the two target entities are replaced by both **X** and **Y**, standing for the first and the second entities of the pair, respectively. Only the context between the two entities are considered. To represent this context, we only take into account lemmas of verbs, common nouns and prepositions. We have observed in preliminary experiments that the performance of the patterns decreased when either these types of lemmas were removed or all lemmas including grammatical words (stop words), adjectives and proper names were retained. It follows that verbs, common nouns and prepositions are critical pieces of information to define the lexico-syntactic contexts of the target terms. Figure 1 contains an example of a pattern associated to the relation `hasBirthplace` (Table 1 also shows a set of extracted patterns in Portuguese).

All the process is performed without human revision. Note that this method may lead us to annotate *false positives* or *false negatives*. However, a manual evaluation on 1000 patterns show that this method has a precision of about 80%.

5.2 Pattern Generalization

We use the following method for making generic patterns, then transformed into high-precision rules:

1. First, we take all the patterns of type "**X**[...]**Y**" and select the most precise ones according to their confidence value. This value is obtained as follows: we calculate the positive and negative frequencies of each pattern; then we subtract the negative frequency from the positive, and sort the patterns by this value. Finally, the top *n* most confident patterns are selected (where $n = 20$ in our experiments). The same process is made for "**Y**[...]**X**" patterns.

2. Then, we apply a generalization algorithm for extracting the longest common string (*lcs*) from these patterns. In order to generalize two patterns, we check first if they are similar and then all those units that they do not share are removed. The similarity, noted $Dice\_lcs$, between two patterns p_1 and p_2 is defined using the longest common string and Dice metric as follows:

$$Dice\_lcs(p_1, p_2) = \frac{2 * lcs(p_1, p_2)}{length(p_1) + length(p_2)} \quad (4)$$

where $lcs(p_1, p_2)$ is the size of the longest common string between patterns p_1 and p_2, and $length(p_i)$ represents the size of pattern p_i. It means the similarity between two patterns is a function of their longest common string and their lengths.

After computing the similarity between two patterns p_1 and p_2, the *lcs* is extracted if and only if p_2 is the most similar pattern to p_1 and the similarity score is higher than a particular threshold (0.75 in our tests). The longest common string of two patterns is considered as the generalized pattern out of them.

3. We filter out those generalized patterns that are not in the best initial 20 patterns, so we automatically obtain a few set of very confident patterns (see Table 1 for an example).

4. All these generic patterns are added as blocks of rules into a grammar, which already has a set of dependency rules for text compression. The new semantic rules take the first entity **X** as the Head, and the second one **Y** as the Dependent of the relation. This process is made manually.

5. Finally, the grammar is compiled into a parser, which is applied on a corpus to obtain triples "**X** `relation` **Y**".

Table 1 shows an example of pattern generalization, with the best extracted patterns, the generic one automatically obtained as well an extraction rule.

Extracted Patterns: <**X** nascer_V em_PRP **Y**>,
<**X** nascer_V em_PRP a_DA cidade_N de_PRP **Y**>,
<**X** nascer_V em_PRP NP Fc **Y**>,
<**X** Fc_V nascer_V em_PRP **Y**>,
<**X** nascer_V CC residir_V em_PRP **Y**>,
[...]

Generic Pattern: <**X** nascer_V em_PRP **Y**>
Rule: **N<tp:P>** V<l:nascer> [P<l:em>] **N<tp:L>**

Table 1: Example of pattern generalization for the `hasBirthplace` relation in Portuguese (*nascer* means "to be born", *cidade* means "city" and *residir*, "to live").

In sum, the application of the longest common string algorithm on the best extracted patterns allows us to obtain a small set of high-quality rules in a weakly-supervised way. These rules, added at the end of a partial dependency grammar, extract instances of pairs belonging to the initial relation.

6 Experiments

We carried out three major experiments in order to know the performance of our RE method. First, we compared the rule-based approach to two baselines in a manually revised corpus containing examples of the relation `hasProfession` in Spanish. We also compared the performance of the system using a large amount of initial pairs (see Section 5.1) as well as with a small set of seed pairs.

Second, we applied a parser with the obtained extraction rules for the biographical relations `hasProfession` and `hasBirthplace` on the whole Spanish and Portuguese Wikipedias.

Finally, we applied the same Portuguese parser on a journalistic corpus, in order to know the performance on the system in different text genres.

6.1 Initial Data

We first obtained about 10,000 pairs for each relation and language (Portuguese and Spanish) from the Wikipedia infoboxes. Then, we identified near 20,000 sentences containing a personal name and (i) an occupation noun (`hasProfession`) or (ii) a location (`hasBirthplace`), which were automatically classified as positive or negative using the distant-supervision strategy described in Section 5.1. Finally, we randomly selected two sets of 2,000 sentences for each relation and language as well as a small set of 200 for the relation `hasProfession`. The latter set was selected for evaluating the use of a small input.

For testing, we randomly selected 1,000 sentences of `hasProfession` (different from the previous sets), which were manually revised.[2]

6.2 Results

Our first experiment evaluates the performance of the rule-based method compared to two baselines (in Spanish): *Baseline_1* performs a pattern-matching approach applying on the test set the whole positive sentences (except for the proper nouns, replaced by a PoS-tag) from the initial 2,000 set. *Baseline_2* uses the 2,000 initial sentences to train a Support Vector Machine classifier, representing each instance with the `token_TAG` elements as features. For this purpose, we used the WEKA implementation of the SMO algorithm (Witten and Frank, 2005).

To evaluate the rule-based system, we performed two experiments: the first one extracted the rules from the initial 200 sentences (*Rule_1*, with only 2 extraction rules) while the second one used the 2,000 set of sentences (*Rule_2*, with 8 rules). The test only contains the 15 most frequent occupations found in the Wikipedia infoboxes, so the evaluation only takes into account the extraction containing these 15 nouns.

Table 2 shows the results of the four described methods over the test set. Precision is the number of correct positive decisions divided by the number of positive decisions (true and false positives). Recall is the number of correct positive decisions divided by the total of positive examples found in the test.

The pattern-matching baseline (*Baseline_1*) has a precision of 100%, but its f-score is merely 10% due to its low recall values. *Baseline_2* performs better, but it produces many false positives, so its precision values do not achieve 45%.

Both rule-based methods perform clearly better than the proposed baselines. *Rule_1*, with only two generic rules, achieves over 55% recall, maintaining the same precision as the pattern-matching models. The use of more data allowed us to add a set of 8 generic rules, so the *Rule_2* method increased its re-

[2]Both training and testing sets will be avaliable at `http://gramatica.usc.es/pln/`

Model	Precision	Recall	F-score
Baseline_1	100%	5.8%	10.1%
Baseline_2	44.51%	42.54%	43.5%
Rule_1	99.02%	55.8%	71.38%
Rule_2	99.16%	65.2%	**78.7%**

Table 2: Precision, Recall and F-score of the Baselines and the two rule-based models for the `hasProfession` relation in Spanish. Test set of 1,000 sentences.

Language	Relation	Precision	Pairs
Spanish	`hasProf.`	85.35%	241,323
	`hasBirth.`	95.56%	13,083
Portuguese	`hasProf.`	93.86%	17,281
	`hasBirth.`	90.34%	5,762

Table 3: Precision and unique extracted pairs for each relation in the whole Spanish and Portuguese Wikipedias.

call in more than 10% without losing precision.

Since the test sentences used in these experiments were filtered with a small list of frequent occupation nouns, we performed other extractions in order to know the performance of our system in real text conditions. So we used the *Rule_2* method to parse the whole Spanish and Portuguese Wikipedias. For this purpose, we extracted seven `hasProfession` rules for Portuguese. Moreover, we add the `hasBirthplace` rules for each language obtained from the initial 2,000 sets of this relation (four different rules were added for each language). Semantic information obtained from the NEC was used only in those `hasBirthplace` rules that did not have verb lemmas (such as *nacer/nascer*, "to be born").

Before evaluating the extraction in the whole corpora, we automatically remove some noise by eliminating tokens with less than 3 characters or with numbers. `hasProfession` pairs were filtered with the occupation nouns obtained from the Spanish and Portuguese Wikipedia infoboxes (about 500 and 250, respectively). To evaluate the `hasBirthplace` relation, the complete output of the extraction was used. We randomly selected and revised samples of 50 pairs from each rule, and calculate the weighted average of the extraction.

Table 3 shows the results of the two extractions over the Spanish and Portuguese Wikipedias. Only a single parsing was performed for each language (with both `hasProfession` and `hasBirthplace` extraction rules). Note that the corpora have about 3.2 and 1.8 gigabytes for Spanish and Portuguese, respectively.

In Spanish, almost 241,000 unique pairs of `hasProfession` related entities were extracted, and more than 13,000 different instances of `hasBirthplace`. Precision values for the first relation were worse than those obtained in the previous experiment (85% *vs* 99%). However, a deep evaluation of the errors shows that many of them were produced in previous processing steps (namely the identification of proper nouns), so the precision of these rules is likely to be better. `hasBirthplace` had better precision results (95%), but the amount of extracted pairs was noticeably lower.

In Portuguese, the system extracted about 17,000 and 5,700 `hasProfession` and `hasBirthplace` unique pairs, respectively. The differences between the Portuguese and the Spanish extractions have probably several reasons: on the one hand, the size of the Spanish corpus is almost the double. On the other hand, the number of occupation nouns used as a filter was also half in the Portuguese experiments. However, the extractions in Portuguese maintain high-precision values (90-93%).

Note that both `hasBirthplace` and `hasProfession` relations extract biographical data, so it is expected that encyclopedic resources such as Wikipedia contain many instances of these relations. Nevertheless, as we intend to perform extractions on texts of different genres, we applied the same Portuguese parser on a journalistic corpus from Público, a general-purpose Portuguese newspaper (with about 1.2 gigabytes).

In Table 4 we can see the results on the Público newspaper (evaluated in the same way as Wikipedia extractions). The first impression of these data is that the extraction doubles the number of instances with respect to the parsing of Wikipedia (which has a similar size). Precision values are between 6% and 9% lower, achieving 84% in both semantic relations. However, in a quick review of the extracted data, we also noted that many instances were incorrect due to the previous errors cited above.

Relation	Precision	Pairs
hasProfession	84.54%	41,669
hasBirthplace	84.67%	11,842

Table 4: Precision and unique extracted pairs for each relation in the Portuguese newspaper Público.

7 Conclusions

This paper presents a novel weakly-supervised approach for semantic Relation Extraction in different languages. We apply a sort of text compression strategy by means of partial dependency parsing which simplifies the linguistic structures, thus allowing the extraction rules to increase their coverage.

In order to (semi)automatically obtain these rules, we first extract lexico-syntactic patterns using a distant-supervision strategy. These patterns are generalized by a longest common string algorithm and finally transformed into semantic rules added at the end of a formal grammar.

Several experiments in different languages and corpora showed that this method maintains the high-precision values of pattern-matching techniques, while the recall is significantly improved.

In future work, we will carry out further experiments with other relations as well as in different corpora. Moreover, we will analyze the performance of the method with different Named Entity Classifiers, in order to avoid some noise during the extraction. Finally, we intend to take advantage of some anaphora and coreference resolution methods that might allow us to extract a large number of instances and to make a fusion process easier.

Acknowledgments

This work has been supported by the MICINN, within the project with reference FFI2010-14986.

References

Aguado de Cea, G., Gómez Pérez, A., Montiel-Ponsoda, E. and Suárez-Figueroa, M. C. 2009. Using Linguistic Patterns to Enhance Ontology Development. In: *Proceedings of KEOD*, 206–213.

Aussenac-Gilles, N. and Jacques, M.-P. 2006. Designing and Evaluating Patterns for Ontology Enrichment from Texts. In *Proceedings of EKAW*, 158–165.

Bollegala, D. T., Matsuo, Y. and Ishizuka, M. 2010. Relational duality: unsupervised extraction of semantic relations between entities on the web. In: *Proceedings of IW3C2*, 151–160.

Brin, S. 1998. Extracting patterns and relations from the world wide web. In: *WebDB Workshop at EDBT*, 172–183.

Chandrasekar, R., Doran, C. and Srinivas, B. 1996. Motivations and methods for text simplification. In: *Proceedings of COLING*, 2, 1041–1044.

Clarke, J. and Lapata, M. 2006. Models for Sentence Compression: A Comparison across Domains, Training Requirements and Evaluation Measures. In: *Proceedings of COLING/ACL*, 377–384.

Cohn, T. and Lapata, M. 2009. Sentence Compression as Tree Transduction. *Journal of Artificial Intelligence Research*, 34: 637–674.

Etzioni, O., Banko, M., Soderland, S. and Weld, D. S. 2008. Open Information Extraction from the Web. In: *ACM* 51, 12, 68–74.

Gamallo P. and González, I. 2011. A Grammatical Formalism Based on Patterns of Part-of-Speech Tags. *International Journal of Corpus Linguistics*, 16: 1, 45–71.

Hearst, M. A. 1992. Automatic acquisition of hyponyms from large text corpora. In: *Proceedings of COLING*, 2, 539–545.

Hoffmann, R., Zhang, C. and Weld, D.S. 2010. Learning 5000 Relational Extractors In: *Proceedigns of ACL*, 286–295.

Mintz, M., Bills, S., Snow, R. and Jurafsky, D. 2009. Distant supervision for relation extraction without labeled data. In: *Proceedings of ACL/IJCNLP*, 2.

Molina, A., da Cunha, I., Torres-Moreno, J-M. and Velazquez-Morales, P. 2010. La compresión de frases: un recurso para la optimización de resumen automático de documentos. *Linguamática*, 2: 3, 13–27.

Padró, Ll., Collado, M., Reese, S., Lloberes, M. and Castellón, I. 2010. FreeLing 2.1: Five Years of Open-Source Language Processing Tools. In: *Proceedings of LREC*.

Pantel, P. and Pennacchiotti, M. 2006. Espresso: Leveraging Generic Patterns for Automatically Harvesting Semantic Relations. In: *Proceedings of COLING/ACL*, 113–120.

Ravichandran, D. and Hovy, E. 2002. Learning surface text patterns for a question answering system. In: *Proceedings of ACL*, 41–47.

Witten, I. H. and Frank, E. 2005. Data mining: practical machine learning tools and techniques with Java implementations. Elsevier Inc., San Francisco.

Wu, F. and Weld, D. 2010. Open information extraction using Wikipedia. In: *Proceedings of ACL*, 118–127.

How to Distinguish a Kidney Theft from a Death Car? Experiments in Clustering Urban-Legend Texts

Roman Grundkiewicz, Filip Graliński
Adam Mickiewicz University
Faculty of Mathematics and Computer Science
Poznań, Poland
rgrundkiewicz@amu.edu.pl, filipg@amu.edu.pl

Abstract

This paper discusses a system for automatic clustering of urban-legend texts. Urban legend (UL) is a short story set in the present day, believed by its tellers to be true and spreading spontaneously from person to person. A corpus of Polish UL texts was collected from message boards and blogs. Each text was manually assigned to one story type. The aim of the presented system is to reconstruct the manual grouping of texts. It turned out that automatic clustering of UL texts is feasible but it requires techniques different from the ones used for clustering e.g. news articles.

1 Introduction

Urban legend is a short story set in the present day, believed by its tellers to be true and spreading spontaneously from person to person, often including elements of humour, moralizing or horror. Urban legends are a form of modern folklore, just as traditional folk tales were a form of traditional folklore, no wonder they are of great interest to folklorists and other social scientists (Brunvand, 1981). As urban legends (and related rumours) often convey misinformation with regard to controversial issues, they can draw the attention of general public as well[1].

The traditional way of collecting urban legends was to interview informants, to tape-record their narrations and to transcribe the recordings (Brunvand, 1981). With the exponential growth of the Internet, more and more urban-legend texts turn up on message boards or blogs and in social media in general. As the web circulation of legends is much easier to tap than the oral one, it becomes feasible to envisage a system for the machine identification and collection of urban-legend texts. In this paper, we discuss the first steps into the creation of such a system. We concentrate on the task of clustering of urban legends, trying to reproduce automatically the results of manual categorisation of urban-legend texts done by folklorists.

In Sec. 2 a corpus of 697 Polish urban-legend texts is presented. The techniques used in preprocessing the corpus texts are discussed in Sec. 3, whereas the clustering process – in Sec. 4. We present the clustering experiment in Sec. 5 and the results – in Sec. 6.

2 Corpus

The corpus of $N = 697$ Polish urban-legend texts was manually collected from the Web, mainly from message boards and blogs[2]. The corpus was not gathered with the experiments of this study in mind, but rather for the purposes of a web-site dedicated to the collection and documentation of the Polish web folklore[3]. The following techniques were used for the extraction of web pages with urban legends:

1. querying Google search engine with formulaic expressions typical of the genre of urban legends, like *znajomy znajomego* (= *friend of a friend*), *słyszałem taką opowieść* (= *I heard this story*) (Graliński, 2009),
2. given a particular story type and its examples, querying the search engine with various combinations of the keywords specific for the story type, their synonyms and paraphrases,
3. collecting texts and links submitted by readers of the web-site mentioned above,

[1] Snopes.com, an urban legends reference web-site, is ranked #2,650 worldwide by Alexa.com (as of May 3, 2011), see http://www.alexa.com/siteinfo/snopes.com

[2] The corpus is available at http://amu.edu.pl/~filipg/uls.tar.gz

[3] See http://atrapa.net

Proceedings of the Workshop on Information Extraction and Knowledge Acquisition, pages 29–36,
Hissar, Bulgaria, 16 September 2011.

4. analysing backlinks to the web-site mentioned above (a message board post containing an urban legend post is sometimes accompanied by a reply "it was debunked here: [link]" or similar),

5. collecting urban-legend texts occurring on the same web page as a text found using the methods (1)-(4) – e.g. a substantial number of threads like "tell an interesting story", "which urban legends do you know?" or similar were found on various message boards.

The web pages containing urban legends were saved and organised with Firefox Scrapbook add-on[4].

Admittedly, method (2) may be favourable to clustering algorithms. This method, however, accounted for about 30% of texts [5] and, what's more, the synonyms and paraphrases were prepared manually (without using any lexicons), some of them being probably difficult to track by clustering algorithms.

Urban-legend texts were manually categorised into 62 story types, mostly according to (Brunvand, 2002) with the exception of a few Polish legends unknown in the United States. The number of texts in each group varied from 1 to 37.

For the purposes of the experiments described in this paper, each urban legend text was manually delimited and marked. Usually a whole message board or blog post was marked, but sometimes (e.g. when an urban legend was just quoted in a longer post) the selection had to be narrowed down to one or two paragraphs. The problems of automatic text delimitation are disregarded in this paper.

Two sample urban-legend texts (both classified as the *kidney theft* story type) translated into English are provided below. The typographical and spelling errors of the original Polish texts are preserved in translation.

> Well yeah... the story maybe not too real, but that kids' organs are being stolen it's actually true!! More and more crimes of this kind have been reported, for example in the Lodz IKEA there was such a crime, to be more precse a girl was kidnapped from this place where parents leave their kids and go shopping (a mini kids play paradise).Yes the gril was brought back home but without a kidney... She is about 5 years old. And I know that becase this girl is my mom's colleague family... We cannot panic and hide our kids in the corners, or pass on such info via GG [Polish instant messenger] cause no this one's going believe, but we shold talk about such stuf, just as a warning...

> I don't know if you heard about it or not, but I will tell you one story which happened recently in Koszalin. In this city a very large shopping centre- Forum was opened some time ago. And as you know there are lots of people, commotion in such places. And it so happened that a couple with a kid (a girl, I guess she was 5,6 years old I don't know exactly) went missing. And you know they searched the shops etc themselves until in the end they called the police. And they thought was kidnapping, they say they waited for an information on a ransom when the girl was found barely alive without a kidney near Forum. Horrible...; It was a shock to me especially cause I live near Koszalin. I'm 15 myself and I have a little sister of a similar age and I don't know what I'd do if such a thing happened to her... Horrible...[6]

The two texts represents basically the same story of a kidney theft, but they differ considerably in detail and wordings.

A smaller subcorpus of 11 story types and 83 legend texts were used during the development.

Note that the corpus of urban-legend texts can be used for other purposes, e.g. as a story-level paraphrase corpus, as each time a given story is re-told by various people in their own words.

3 Document Representation

For our experiments, we used the standard Vector Space Model (VSM), in which each document

[4]http://amb.vis.ne.jp/mozilla/scrapbook/

[5]The exact percentage is difficult to establish, as information on which particular method led to which text was not-saved.

[6]The original Polish text: http://www.samosia.pl/pokaz/341160/jestem_przerazona_jak_mozna_komus_podwedzic_dziecko_i_wyciac_mu_nerke_w_ch

is represented as a vector in a multidimensional space. The selection of terms, each corresponding to a dimension, often depends on a distinctive nature of texts. In this section, we describe some text processing methods, the aim of which is to increase similarity of documents of related topics (i.e. urban legends of the same story type) and decrease similarity of documents of different topics.

3.1 Stop Words

A list of standard Polish stop words (function words, most frequent words etc.) was used during the normalization. The stop list was obtained by combining various resources available on the Internet[7]. The final stop list contained 642 words.

We decided to expand the stop list with some domain-specific and non-standard types of words.

3.1.1 Internet Slang Words

Most of the urban-legend texts were taken from message boards, no wonder Internet slang was used in many of them. Therefore the most popular slang abbreviations, emoticons and onomatopoeic expressions (e.g. *lol, rotfl, btw, xD, hahaha*) were added to the stoplist.

3.1.2 Abstract Verbs

Abstract verbs (i.e. verbs referring to abstract activities, states and concepts rather than to the manipulation of physical objects) seem to be irrelevant for the recognition of the story type of a given legend text. A list of 379 abstract verbs was created automatically using the lexicon of the Polish-English rule-based machine translation system Translatica[8] and taking the verbs with subordinate clauses specified in their valency frames. This way, verbs such as *mówić* (= *say*), *opowiadać* (= *tell*), *pytać* (= *to ask*), *decydować* (= *decide*) could be added to the stop list.

3.1.3 Unwanted Adverbs

A list of Polish intensifiers, quantifiers and sentence-level adverbs was taken from the same lexicon as for the abstract verbs. 536 adverbs were added to the stop list in this manner.

3.1.4 Genre-specific Words

Some words are likely to occur in any text of the given domain, regardless of the specific topic. For example in a mathematical text one can expect words like *function, theorem, equation,* etc. to occur, no matter which topic, i.e. branch of mathematics (algebra, geometry or mathematical analysis), is involved.

Construction of the domain keywords list based on words frequencies in the collection of documents may be insufficient. An external, human knowledge might be used for specifying such words. We decided to add the words specific to the genre of urban legends, such as:

- words expressing family and interpersonal relations, such as *znajomy* (= *friend*), *kolega* (= *colleague*), *kuzyn* (= *cousin*) (urban legends are usually claimed to happen to *a friend of a friend, a cousin of a colleague* etc.),
- words naming the genre of urban legends and similar genres, e.g. *legenda* (= *legend*), *anegdota* (= *anecdote*), *historia* (= *story*),
- words expressing the notions of authenticity or inauthenticity, e.g. *fakt* (= *fact*), *autentyczny* (= *authentic*), *prawdziwy* (= *real*), as they are crucial for the definition of the genre.

3.2 Spell Checking

As very informal style of communication is common on message boards and even blogs, a large number of typographical and spelling errors were found in the collected urban-legend texts. The Hunspell spell checker was used to find misspelled words and generate lists of correction suggestions. Unfortunately, the order in which Hunspell presents its suggestions is of no significance, and consequently it is not trivial to choose the right correction. We used the observation that it is quite likely for the right correction to occur in the corpus and we simply selected the Hunspell suggestion that is the most frequent in the whole corpus. This simple method turned out to be fast and good enough for our application.

3.3 Lemmatisation and stemming

For the lemmatisation and stemming *morfologik-stemming* package[9] was used. This tool is based on an extensive lexicon of Polish inflected forms (as Polish is a language of rather complex inflection rules, there is no simple stemming algorithm as effective as Porter's algorithm for English (Porter, 1980).)

[7] http://www.ranks.nl/stopwords/polish.html, http://pl.wikipedia.org/wiki/Wikipedia:Stopwords

[8] http://poleng.pl/poleng/en/node/597

[9] http://morfologik.blogspot.com/

3.4 Use of Thesaurus

A thesaurus of synonyms and near-synonyms might be used in order to increase the quality of the distance measure between documents. However, in case of polysemous words word-sense disambiguation would be required. As no WSD system for Polish was available we decided to adopt a naive approach of constructing a smaller thesaurus containing only unambiguous words.

As the conversion of diminutives and augmentatives to forms from which they were derived can be regarded as a rather safe normalisation, i.e. there are not many problematic diminutives or augmentatives, such derivations were taken into account during the normalisation. Note that diminutive forms can be created for many Polish words (especially for nouns) and are very common in the colloquial language.

A list of Polish diminutives and augmentatives has been created from a dump of Wiktionary[10] pages. The whole list included above 5.5 thousand sets of words along with their diminutives and augmentatives.

4 Document Clustering

The task of document clustering consists in recognising topics in a document collection and dividing documents according to some similarity measure into K clusters. Representing documents in a multi-dimensional space makes it possible to use well-known general-purpose clustering algorithms.

4.1 Clustering Algorithms

K-Means (KM) (Jain et al., 1999; Berkhin, 2002; Manning et al., 2009) is the most widely used flat partitioning clustering algorithm. It seeks to minimise the average squared distances between objects in the same cluster:

$$RSS(K) = \sum_{k=1}^{K} \sum_{\vec{x}_i \in C_k} \|\vec{x}_i - \vec{c}_k\|^2 \qquad (1)$$

in subsequent iterations until a convergence criterion is met. The $\vec{x}_i$ value means the vector representing the ith document from collection, and $\vec{c}_k$ means the centroid of the kth cluster. There is, however, no guarantee that the global optimum is reached – the result depends on the selection of initial cluster centres (this issue is discussed in Sec. 4.2).

In all of our tests, K-Means turned out to be less efficient than the algorithm known as **K-Medoids** (KMd). K-Medoids uses medoids (the most centrally located objects of clusters) instead of centroids. This method is more robust to noise and outliers than K-Means. The simplest implementation involves the selection of a medoid as the document closest to the centroid of a given cluster.

We examined also popular agglomerative hierarchical clustering algorithms: **Complete Linkage** (CmpL), **Average Linkage** (AvL), known as UPGMA, and **Weighted Average Linkage** (Jain et al., 1999; Berkhin, 2002; Manning et al., 2009). These algorithms differ in how the distance between clusters is determined: in Complete Linkage it is the maximum distance between two documents included in the two groups being compared, whereas in Average Linkage – the average distance, whereas in the last one, distances are weighted based on the number of documents in each of them. It is often claimed that hierarchical methods produce better partitioning than flat methods (Manning et al., 2009). Other agglomerative hierarchical algorithms with various linkage criteria that we tested (i.e. Single Linkage, Centroid Linkage, Median Linkage and Ward Linkage), were outperformed by the ones described above.

We tested also other types of known clustering algorithms. Divisive hierarchical algorithm Bisecting K-Means and fuzzy algorithms as Fuzzy K-means, Fuzzy K-medoids and K-Harmonic Means were far less satisfactory. Moreover, in the case of fuzzy methods it is difficult to determine the fuzziness coefficient.

4.2 Finding the Optimal Seeds

One of the disadvantages of K-means algorithm is that it heavily depends on the selection of initial centroids. Furthermore, the random selection makes algorithm non-deterministic, which is not always desired. Many methods have been proposed for optimal seeds selection (Peterson et al., 2010).

One of the methods which can be used in order to select good seeds and improve flat clustering algorithms is **K-Means++** (KMpp) (Arthur and Vassilvitskii, 2007). Only the first cluster centre is selected uniformly at random in this method,

[10] Polish version of Wiktionary: `http://pl.wiktionary.org/wiki/`

each subsequent seed is chosen from among the remaining objects with probability proportional to the second power of its distance to its closest cluster centre. K-Means++ simply extends the standard K-Means algorithm with a more careful seeding schema, hence an analogous K-Medoids++ (KMdpp) algorithm can be easily created. Note that K-Means++ and K-Medoids++ are still non-deterministic.

We propose yet another approach to solving seeding problem, namely **centres selection by reduction of similarities (RS)**. The goal of this technique is to select the K-element subset with the highest overall dissimilarity. The reduction of similarities consists in the following steps:

1. Specify the number of initial cluster centres (K).
2. Find the most similar pair of documents in the document set.
3. Out of the documents of the selected pair, remove the one with the highest sum of similarities to other documents.
4. If the number of remaining documents equals K then go to step 5, else go to step 2.
5. The remaining documents will be used as initial cluster centres.

The simplest implementation can be based on the similarity matrix of documents. In our experiments reduction of similarities provided a significant improvement in the efficiency of clusters initialisation process (even though the $N-K$ steps need to be performed – for better efficiency, a random sample of data could be used). It may also cause that the outliers will be selected as seeds, so much better results are obtained with combination with the K-Medoids algorithm.

The best result for flat clustering methods in general was obtained with K-Medoids++ algorithm (see Sec. 6), it has to be, however, restarted a number of times to achieve good results and is non-deterministic.

4.3 Cluster Cardinality

Many clustering algorithms require the *a priori* specification of the number of clusters K. Several algorithms and techniques have been created to determine the optimal value of K automatically (Milligan and Cooper, 1985; Likas et al., 2001; Feng and Hamerly, 2007).

For K-means, we can use a heuristic method for choosing K according to the objective function. Define $RSS_{\min}(K)$ as the minimal RSS (see eq. 1) of all clusterings with the K clusters, which can be estimated by applying reduction of similarities technique. The point at which $RSS_{\min}(K)$ graph flattens may indicate the optimal value of K.

If we can make the assumption that $RSS_{\min}$ values are obtained through the RS, we can find the flattenings very fast and quite accurate. Moreover, the deterministic feature of the introduced method favours this assumption. Starting from the calculations of the $RSS_{\min}$ value for the largest K, we do not have to run the RS technique anew in the each next step. For $K-1$ it is sufficient to remove only one centroid from K previously selected, thus the significant increase in performance is achieved.

4.4 Evaluation Method

Purity measure is a simple external evaluation method derived from information retrieval (Manning et al., 2009). In order to compute purity, in each cluster the number of documents assigned to the most frequent class in the given cluster is calculated, and then sum of these counts is divided by the number of all documents (N):

$$purity(C, L) = \frac{1}{N} \sum_{k} \max_{j} \mid C_k \cap L_j \mid \quad (2)$$

where $L = \{L_1, \ldots, L_m\}$ is the set of the (expected) classes.

The main limitation of purity is that it gives poor results when the number of clusters is different from the real number of valid classes. Purity can give irrelevant values if the classes significantly differ in size and larger ones are divided into smaller clusters. This is because the same class may be recognized as the most numerous in the two or more clusters.

We propose a simple modification to purity that helps to avoid such situations: let each cluster be assigned to the class which is the most frequent in a given cluster and only if this class is the most numerous in this cluster among all the clusters.

Hence, each class is counted only once (for a cluster in which it occurs most frequently) and some of the clusters can be assigned to no class. This method of evaluation will be called **strict purity measure**. The value of strict purity is less than or equal to the standard purity calculated on the same partition.

5 Experiment Settings

To measure the distance between two documents d_i and d_j we used the cosine similarity defined as the cosine of the angle between their vectors:

$$sim_{\cos}(d_i, d_j) = \frac{\vec{d_i} \cdot \vec{d_j}}{\|\vec{d_i}\| \|\vec{d_j}\|} \quad (3)$$

The standard tf-idf weighting scheme was used.

Other types of distance measures and weighting models were considered as well, but preliminary tests showed that this setting is sufficient.

Table 1 presents text normalisations used in the experiment. Natural initial normalisations are `d,ch,m`, i.e.: (1) lowercasing all words (this ensures proper recognition of the words at the beginning of a sentence), (2) spell checking and (3) stemming using Morfologik package. All subsequent normalizations mentioned in this paper will be preceded by this initial sequence.

Symbol	Explanation
`ss`	Cut words after the sixth character
`m`	Stemming with Morfologik package
`ch`	Spell checking with Hunspell
`d`	Lowercase all words
`rs`	Remove only simple stop words
`rl`	Remove genre specific words
`rc`	Remove Polish city names
`p`	Remove stop words with abstract verbs, unwanted adverbs and Internet slang words
`t`	Use thesaurus to normalise synonyms, diminutives and augmentatives

Table 1: Text normalisations used.

6 Results

We compared a number of seeds selection techniques for the flat clustering algorithms using the smaller sub-corpus of 83 urban-legend texts. The results suggested that the K-Medoids++ and K-Medoids combined with centres selection by reduction of similarities perform better than other methods (see Table 2). The algorithms that are non-deterministic were run five times and the maximum values were taken. The best result for the development sub-corpus was obtained using Average Linking with the normalisation without any thesaurus.

Alg.	Purity	P_{strict}	Purity	P_{strict}
	`rs,t`		`p,rl,t`	
KM	0.783	0.675	0.762	0.711
KMd	0.831	0.759	0.871	0.847
KMpp	0.916	0.904	0.952	0.94
KMdpp	**0.988**	**0.976**	**0.988**	**0.976**
KM_{RS}	0.807	0.759	0.964	0.94
KMd_{RS}	0.965	0.918	**0.988**	**0.976**

Table 2: Comparison of flat clustering algorithms using the development set.

Results obtained for the test corpus are presented in Table 3. All tests were performed for the natural number of clusters ($K = 62$). Hierarchical methods proved to be more effective than flat clustering algorithms probably because the former do not seek equal-sized clusters. The best strict purity value (0.825) was achieved for the Average Linkage algorithm with the `p,rl,t,ss` normalisation. Average Linking was generally better than the other methods and gave results above 0.8 for the simplest text normalisation as well.

For the best result obtained, 22 clusters (35.5%) were correct and 5 clusters (8%) contained one text of an incorrect story type or did not contain one relevant text. For 10 classes (16%) two similar story types were merged into one cluster (e.g. two stories about dead pets: *the dead pet in the package* and *"undead" dead pet*). Only one story type was divided into two "pure" clusters (shorter versions of a legend were categorised into a separate group). The worst case was the *semen in fast food* story type, for which 31 texts were divided into 5 different clusters. A number of singleton clusters with outliers was also formed.

As far as flat algorithms are concerned, K-Medoids++ gave better results, close to the best results obtained with Average Linkage[11]. The

[11]The decrease in the clusters quality after adding some normalisation to K-Medoids++ algorithm, does not necessar-

value of 0.821 was, however, obtained with different normalisations including simple stemming. K-Medoids with reduction of similarities gave worse results but was about four times faster than K-Medoids++.

Both flat and hierarchical algorithms did not manage to handle the correct detection of small classes, although it seems that words unique to each of them could be identified. For example, often merged story types about student exams: *a pimp* (11 texts) and *four students* (4 texts) contain words *student* (= *student*), *profesor* (= *professor*) and *egzamin* (= *exam*), but only the former contains words *alfons* (= *pimp*), *dwója* (= *failing mark*), whereas *samochód* (= *car*), *koło* (= *wheel*) and *jutro* (= *tomorrow*) occur only in the latter. Similarly, topics *fishmac* (7) and *have you ever caught all the fish?* (3) contain word *ryba* (= *fish*) but the first one is about McDonald's burgers and the second one is a police joke. In addition, texts of both story types are very short.

Hierarchical methods produced more singleton clusters (including incorrect clusters), though K-Medoids can also detect true singleton classes as *in a willy* and *dad peeing into a sink*. These short legends consist mainly of a dialogue and seem to be dissimilar to others, so they have often been taken as initial centroids in K-Medoids$_{RS}$ and K-Medoids++. Topics containing texts of similar length are handled better, even if they are very numerous, e.g. *what is Your name?* (32). But this legend is very simple and has few variants. On the other hand, the popular legend *semen in fast food* (31) has many variants (as semen is allegedly found in a milkshake, kebab, hamburger, salad etc.).

The results confirm the validity of the proposed text normalisation techniques: better clusters are obtained after removing the non-standard types of words and with a thesaurus including diminutives and augmentatives. Further development of the thesaurus may lead to the increase of the clusters quality.

6.1 Guessing Cluster Cardinality

Fig. 1 presents the estimated minimal average sum of squares as a function of the number of clusters K for K-Medoids with centres selection by the RS

ily imply the worse effectiveness, but may suggest an unfortunate random selection of the first centroid.

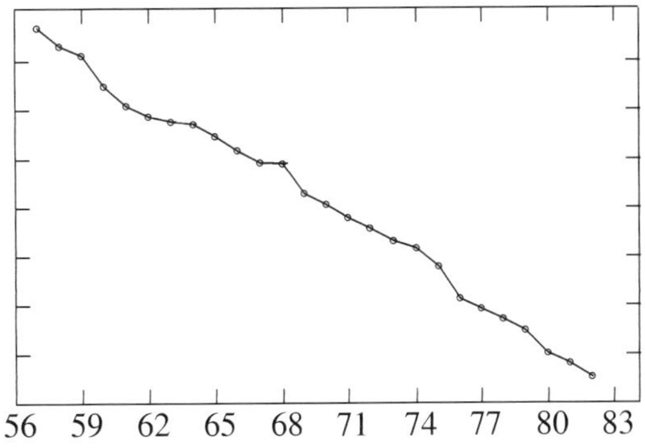

Figure 1: Sum of squares as a function of the K value in K-Medoids with seeds selection by reduction of similarities. Used normalization: `p,rl,t,td,ss`.

(i.e. minimal values of the $RSS(K)$ for each K is approximated with this technique). The most probably natural number of clusters is 67, which is not much larger than the correct number (62), and the next ones are 76 and 69. It comes as no surprise as for $K = 62$ many classes were incorrectly merged (rather than divided into smaller ones). The most probable number of guessed cluster cardinality would not change a wider range of K than one presented in Fig. 1 if were considered.

7 Conclusions

The clustering of urban-legend texts should be considered harder than e.g. clustering of news articles:

- An urban-legend text of the same story type may take very different forms, sometimes the story is summarised in just one sentence, sometimes it is a detailed retelling.
- Other legends are sometimes alluded to in a text of a given story type.
- The frequency of named entities in urban-legend texts is rather low. City names are sometimes used but taking them into account does not help much, if any (legends are rarely tied to a specific place or city, they usually "happen" where the story-teller lives). Hence it is not possible to base the clustering on named entities like in case of the news clustering (Toda and Kataoka, 2005).

Normalization	Words	KMd	KMd$_{RS}$	KMdpp	CmpL	AvL	WAvL
rs	7630	0.675	0.732	0.771	0.747	0.806	0.798
rs,rl	7583	0.694	0.742	0.776	0.772	0.789	0.776
rs,t	6259	0.699	0.743	0.805	0.779	0.799	0.766
rs,rl,t	6237	0.688	0.731	0.775	0.818	0.785	0.770
p,rl	7175	0.698	0.743	0.773	0.77	0.78	0.798
p,rl,rc	7133	0.697	0.739	0.794	0.773	0.758	0.795
p,rl,ss	6220	0.684	0.763	0.758	0.750	0.808	0.792
p,rl,t	5992	0.699	0.732	0.786*	0.806	**0.825**	0.778
p,rl,t,rc	5957	0.618	0.731	0.777	0.811	0.824	0.776
p,rl,t,ss	5366	0.719	0.775	**0.821***	0.789	0.813*	0.791
p,rl,t,rc,ss	5340	0.71	0.786	0.775	0.789	0.811	0.791
Mean	—	0.689	0.747	0.783	0.782	0.8	0.785

Table 3: Results of clustering urban-legend texts (strict purity) for algorithms: K-Medoids (KMd), K-Medoids++ (KMdpp), K-Medoids with seeds selection (KMd$_{RS}$), Complete Linkage (CmpL), Average Linkage (AvL) and Weighted Average Linkage (WAvL). Values with the star sign were obtained with the probabilistic document frequency instead of the idf.

- Some story types include the same motif, e.g. texts of distinct story types used the same motif of laughing paramedics dropping a trolley with a patient.
- Urban legends as texts extracted from the Internet contain a large number of typographical and spelling errors.

Similar problems will be encountered when building a system for discovering new urban-legend texts and story types.

Acknowledgement

The paper is based on research funded by the Polish Ministry of Science and Higher Education (Grant No N N516 480540).

References

David Arthur and Sergei Vassilvitskii. 2007. *k-means++: The advantages of careful seeding.* SODA 2007: Proceedings of the eighteenth annual ACM-SIAM symposium on Discrete algorithms, 1027–1035.

Pavel Berkhin. 2002. *Survey Of Clustering Data Mining Techniques.* Accrue Software, San Jose, CA.

Jan H. Brunvand. 1981. *The vanishing hitchhiker: American urban legends and their meanings*, Norton.

Jan H. Brunvand. 2002. *Encyclopedia of Urban Legends*, Norton.

Yu Feng and Greg Hamerly. 2007. *PG-means: learning the number of clusters in data.* Advances in Neural Information Processing Systems 19, 393–400, MIT Press.

Filip Graliński. 2009 *Legendy miejskie w internecie.* Mity współczesne. Socjologiczna analiza współczesnej rzeczywistości kulturowej, 175–186, Wydawnictwo Akademii Techniczno-Humanistycznej w Bielsku-Białej.

Anil K. Jain, M. Narasimha Murty and Patrick J. Flynn. 1999. *Data Clustering: A Review.* ACM Computing Survey, 31, 264–323.

Aristidis Likas, Nikos Vlassis and Jakob J. Verbeek. 2001. *The Global K-Means Clustering Algorithm.* Pattern Recognition, 36, 451–461.

Christopher D. Manning, Prabhakar Raghavan and Hinrich Schütze. 2009. *An Introduction to Information Retrieval.* Cambridge University Press.

Glenn W. Milligan and Martha C. Cooper. 1985. *An examination of procedures for determining the number of clusters in a data set.* Psychometrika.

Anna D. Peterson, Arka P. Ghosh and Ranjan Maitra. 2010. *A systematic evaluation of different methods for initializing the K-means clustering algorithm.* Transactions on Knowledge and Data Engineering.

Martin F. Porter. 1980. *An algorithm for suffix stripping.* Program, 3, 130–137, Morgan Kaufmann Publishers Inc.14.

Hiroyuki Toda and Ryoji Kataoka. 2005. *A clustering method for news articles retrieval system.* Special interest tracks and posters of the 14th international conference on WWW, ACM, 988–989.

Machine Reading Between the Lines: A Simple Evaluation Framework for Extracted Knowledge Bases

Avirup Sil and **Alexander Yates**
Center for Data Analytics and Biomedical Informatics
Temple University
Broad St. and Montgomery Ave.
Philadelphia, PA 19122
{avirup.sil, yates}@temple.edu

Abstract

The traditional method to evaluate a knowledge extraction system is to measure precision and recall. But this method only partially measures the quality of a knowledge base (KB) as it cannot predict whether a KB is *useful* or not. One of the ways in which a KB can be useful is if it is able to deduce implicit information from text which standard information extraction techniques cannot extract. We propose a novel, simple evaluation framework called "Machine Reading between the Lines" (MRbtL) which measures the usefulness of extracted KBs by determining how much they can help improve a relation extraction system. In our experiments, we compare two KBs which both have high precision and recall according to annotators who evaluate the knowledge in the KBs independently from any application or context. But, we show that one outperforms the other in terms of MRbtL experiments, as it can accurately deduce more new facts from the output of a relation extractor more accurately. In short, one extracted KB can read between the lines to identify extra information, whereas the other one cannot.

1 Introduction

Evaluating knowledge bases (KBs), and especially extracted KBs can be difficult. Researchers typically measure the accuracy of extracted KBs by measuring precision and recall. But this only partially measures the value of a KB. Size and correctness are important intrinsic measures, but a KB that states "1 is an integer, 2 is an integer, ..." contains an infinite number of correct facts, but is not very useful for most tasks. Researchers have proposed a variety of applications as testbeds for evaluating the *usefulness* of knowledge bases, and the Recognizing Textual Entailment Challenge (Dagan et al., 2006) has received increasing attention as an interesting testbed (Clark et al., 2007). However, evaluating a knowledge base on RTE requires implementing a functioning RTE system, which is in itself a nontrivial task. Furthermore, even if a particular kind of knowledge could be useful for RTE, it may not help improve an RTE system's score unless all of the other knowledge required for the complex inferences in this task are already present. In short, an effective KB evaluation framework is one that:

- is easy to implement
- is able to measure a KB's utility on a valued application such as relation extraction

In response, we propose a task called "Machine Reading between the Lines" (MRbtL). In this task, a relation extraction system first extracts a base set of facts from a corpus. An extracted KB is then used to deduce new facts from the output of the relation extractor. The KB is evaluated on the precision and amount of "new" facts that can be inferred.

We also argue that MRbtL evaluation is more rigorous than asking an annotator to evaluate the usefulness of a stand-alone piece of knowledge, because it forces the annotator to consider the application of the knowledge in a specific context. In addition, success on MRbtL provides an immediate benefit to relation extraction, an area which many NLP practitioners care about.

2 Previous Work

The MRbtL task is similar in spirit to the vision of Peñas and Hovy (2010), but they focus on a background knowledge about the names for relations between two nouns. MRbtL also provides a

Proceedings of the Workshop on Information Extraction and Knowledge Acquisition, pages 37–40,
Hissar, Bulgaria, 16 September 2011.

quantitative evaluation framework for the implicit extractions which is missing from the Peñas and Hovy work. Goyal *et al.* (2010) present a system for annotating stories with information about whether specific events are positive or negative for characters in the story. Viewed as an MRbtL task, they extract knowledge about whether actions and events cause people to be happy or unhappy, a very specific kind of knowledge. They then implement an inference technique, much more sophisticated than our variable substitution method, for applying this specific extracted knowledge to stories.

3 Machine Reading between the Lines

Let us assume that we have a knowledge base KB and a corpus C from which a Machine Reading or information extraction system has extracted a database of relational extractions (RE). In the MRbtL framework, a KB is evaluated on the set of additional ground extractions, called *implicit extractions* (IE) which are entailed by the KB: $KB \wedge RE \models IE$. MRbtL systems are then judged on the precision, amount, and *redundancy* of IE. By redundancy, we mean the fraction of extracted knowledge in IE that overlaps with RE, or is obvious *a priori*. If IE is *accurate* and contains many non-redundant extractions, then we judge KB to be a useful knowledge base. The advantage of this setup is that a system's score on the task depends only on the KB, a relation extractor, and a simple logical inference engine for performing variable substitutions and *modus ponens*. These last two are often freely available or quite cheap to build. Formally, our three evaluation metrics are defined as follows:

$$Accuracy : \frac{|\text{ Correct Extractions in } IE\ |}{|IE|}$$

$$Amount : |IE|$$

$$Redundancy : \frac{|IE \cap RE|}{|IE|}$$

Consider a very simple knowledge base which extracts knowledge about the President of a country. It has an axiom: $\forall_{p,c} president\_of(p,c) \Rightarrow person(p) \wedge country(c)$. Using this axiom, a relation extraction system can extract $president\_of(Obama, USA)$ which would then belong to RE. If RE also contains $person(Obama)$ extracted separately from the same sentence or document, then this extraction would be correct but redundant.

4 Evaluating Two STRIPS KBs with MRbtL

Common-sense knowledge about the changes in the state of the world over time is one of the most crucial forms of knowledge for an intelligent agent, since it informs an agent of the ways in which it can act upon the world. A recent survey of the common-sense knowledge involved in the recognizing textual entailment task demonstrates that knowledge about action and event semantics, in particular, constitutes a major component of the knowledge involved in understanding natural language (LoBue and Yates, 2011). In this section, we describe two example KBs of action and event semantics extracted by our previous work and also discuss an evaluation of these KBs using MRbtL.

We define *actions* as observable phenomena, or *events*, that are brought about by rational agents. One of the best-known, and still widely used, representations for action semantics is the STRIPS representation (Fikes and Nilsson, 1971). Formally, a STRIPS representation is a 5-tuple $(a, args, pre, add, del)$ consisting of the action name a, a list $args$ of argument variables that range over the set of objects in the world, and three sets of predicates that reference the argument variables. The first, the *precondition* list pre, is a set of conditions that must be met in order for the action to be allowed to take place. For instance, in order for someone to *awaken*, she or he must first be *asleep*. The other two sets of conditions specify how the world changes when the action takes place: the add list describes the set of new conditions that must be true afterwards (*e.g.*, after the event *insert(pencil24,sharpener3)*, *in(pencil24,sharpener3)* holds true), and the del list specifies the conditions that were true before the action happened but are no longer true. These add and del conditions are sometimes collectively referred to as *effects* or *postconditions*.

Formally, the precondition, add and delete lists correspond to a set of rules describing the logical consequence of observing an event. Let t_1 be the time point immediately preceding an event e with arguments **args**, t_2 the time of event e, and t_3 the time immediately following e. For each precondition p, each add effect a, and each delete effect d, the following rules hold:

$$\forall_{\mathbf{args}} e(\mathbf{args}, t_2) \Rightarrow p(\mathbf{args}_p, t_1)$$
$$\forall_{\mathbf{args}} e(\mathbf{args}, t_2) \Rightarrow a(\mathbf{args}_a, t_3) \quad (1)$$
$$\forall_{\mathbf{args}} e(\mathbf{args}, t_2) \Rightarrow \neg d(\mathbf{args}_d, t_3)$$

where $\mathbf{args}_x$ represents the subset of the arguments to which the predicate x applies.

4.1 Two extracted STRIPS KBs

We earlier introduced two different KBs that extract preconditions and postconditions (add and delete effects) of actions. One of the KBs (Sil et al., 2010) (henceforth, S10) uses candidate pre and postconditions which have high pointwise mutual information (PMI) with the action words. Given a corpus where each document contains an event e, S10 begins by identifying relations and arguments in a large text corpus using an open-domain semantic role labeler and OpenNLP's noun-phrase coreference resolution system[1]. Taking a set of candidate predicate words, we then define different features of the labeled corpus that measure the proximity in the annotated corpus between a candidate word and the action word. Using a small sample of labeled action words with their correct preconditions and effects, we then train an RBF-kernel Support Vector Machine (SVM) to rank the candidate predicate words by their proximity to the action word.

But, S10 does not generalize adequately *e.g.* it extracts *hammer* as a precondition for the action *crush*. While it is true that if one has a hammer, then one can crush things, this is too strict of a precondition. Hence, we introduce another KB, HYPER (Sil and Yates, 2011), which adds generality to the extractions. HYPER uses Wordnet superclasses as additional candidates (potential pre and postconditions) of actions. Figure 1 shows sample STRIPS extractions from S10 and HYPER.

4.2 MRbtL for S10 and HYPER

We now describe how we can build a MRbtL system for the extracted STRIPS representations. We use the set of predicates and their arguments discovered by the semantic role labeler used by S10 as explicit relational extractions RE; a number of off-the-shelf extractors are available for this purpose. Next, for each occurrence of one of the action words as a predicate in the corpus, we apply the axioms (1) and the knowledge in the S10 and HYPER KBs to deduce predicates that must be true immediately before or after the occurrence of the action. For example, the semantic role labeler discovers the formula *draining*$(a_0, a_1) \wedge$ *the acid solution*(a_1) from the sentence, "This is done by inverting the battery and draining the acid solution out the vent holes in the battery cover". By applying the extracted precondition that the second argument of a *draining* event must be a liquid, we can infer that *liquid*(a_1) is true immediately before the event. Since our MRbtL setup extracts tens of thousands of implicit facts, we evaluate precision and redundancy on samples.

[1] http://opennlp.sourceforge.net

	amputate	crush
args:	x, y	o, p
pre:	organism#1(x), body_part#1(y), has(x, y)	object#1(o), object#1(p), whole(p)
add:	$\neg$has(x, y)	$\neg$whole(p)
del:	has(x, y)	whole(p)
args:	a, b	m, n
pre:	person(a), legs(b), has(a, b)	hammer(m), ice(n), whole(n)
add:	$\neg$has(a, b)	$\neg$whole(n)

Figure 1: **Two example STRIPS representations extracted by the HYPER system (above), and representations for the same actions extracted by our prior work, S10 (below).** In contrast with S10, the HYPER representations require extracting delete effects. Also, HYPER disambiguates and generalizes predicates by identifying WordNet synsets for predicate names. Here, *organism* and *object* (in HYPER) are hypernyms of *person* and *hammer* (in S10) respectively.

5 Experiments

We perform MRbtL experiments on extractions from S10 and HYPER. S10 uses a dataset of 40 actions from the lexical units in the frames that inherit from the *Transitive_action* frame in FrameNet. The document collection has 15,088 documents downloaded from the Web for the 40 action words. We use the annotated Web corpus for HYPER with semantic role information. We measure the quality of our implicit extractions by taking a random sample of 100 and having two judges classify each extraction for accuracy and redundancy (as per the definitions in Sec 3) in the context of the sentence and document from which it was extracted. As per our earlier work, the pre-

	S10	HYPER	κ	signif.
accur.	45%	**73%**	0.65	$p < 0.01$
redun.	21%	**12%**	0.91	$p = .13$
num.	54,300	**67,192**	N/A	N/A

Table 1: **The knowledge base extracted by HYPER can identify more, and more accurate, implicit extractions than S10's knowledge base, and fewer implicit extractions overlap with explicit extractions.** The first two columns record the accuracy and redundancy (averaged over two annotators on sample of 100), and total number of implicit extractions. κ indicates Cohen's κ inter-annotator agreement score, and p-values for the significance tests are calculated using a two-sided Fisher's exact test.

cision of S10 is 93% at 85% recall, whereas for HYPER the precision is 89% at 90% recall. At a first glance, both of the systems look impressive to someone by just looking at the precision/recall numbers.

Table 1 shows the results of our Machine Reading between the Lines experiment. These extractions are based on 15,000 occurrences of the 40 action words, but as we scale the extractors to new action words, we should increasingly be able to read between the lines of texts. Hence, we observe that even when both S10 and HYPER report similar (and high) precision and recall, they report significantly different scores on MRbtL experiments. From Table 1, we clearly see that HYPER outperforms S10. HYPER's implicit extractions are nearly 30% more accurate than S10's, and roughly half as redundant. Extrapolating from the accuracy and redundancy scores in the evaluated sample, HYPER extracts 41,659 correct, non-redundant relationships compared with 7602 extractions for S10 from the Web corpus that does not appear explicitly in the documents.

Example extractions indicate that HYPER's stronger performance on MRbtL is because its extracted pre and postconditions generalize to hypernyms. From the sentence "Doctors need to heal patients..", HYPER extracts *medical_practitioner(doctors)* indicating that *doctors* are of type *medical_practitioner* which is an accurate and non-redundant extraction. Here, *medical_practitioner* is a precondition for action *heal*. But S10 concludes that *doctors* are of type *doctor* (a Wordnet subclass of *medical_practitioner*) which is a redundant extraction. Another example: from the sentence "When a sharp object, like a fingernail or thorn, scrapes along your skin ...", the MRbtL system extracted that the fingernail is an object, since the instrument of a scraping action needs to be an object. Both annotators considered this extraction correct, but redundant, since the sentence explicitly mentions that a fingernail is a kind of object.

6 Conclusion and Future Work

We show that the extracted knowledge base can be used to accurately identify information in a document that is never stated explicitly. We call this evaluation scenario "Machine Reading between the Lines". We demonstrate that HYPER's extracted knowledge base outperforms the closest comparable one though both perform extremely well when measured under only precision and recall. A future direction includes comparing very different KBs with MRbtL.

References

Peter Clark, William R. Murray, John Thompson, Phil Harrison, Jerry Hobbs, and Christiane Fellbaum. 2007. On the role of lexical and world knowledge in rte3. In *Proceedings of the ACL-PASCAL Workshop on Textual Entailment and Paraphrasing*, RTE '07, pages 54–59, Morristown, NJ, USA. Association for Computational Linguistics.

I. Dagan, O. Glickman, and B. Magnini. 2006. The PASCAL Recognising Textual Entailment Challenge. *Lecture Notes in Computer Science*, 3944:177–190.

R. Fikes and N. Nilsson. 1971. STRIPS: A new approach to the application of theorem proving to problem solving. *Artificial Intelligence*, 2(3/4):189–208.

Amit Goyal, Ellen Riloff, and Hal Daumé III. 2010. Automatically producing plot unit representations for narrative text. In *EMNLP*.

Peter LoBue and Alexander Yates. 2011. Types of common-sense knowledge needed for recognizing textual entailment. In *ACL*.

Anselmo Pe nas and Eduard Hovy. 2010. Semantic enrichment of text with background knowledge. In *Proceedings of the NAACL Workshop(FAM-LbR)*.

Avirup Sil and Alexander Yates. 2011. Extracting strips representations of actions and events. In *RANLP*.

Avirup Sil, Fei Huang, and Alexander Yates. 2010. Extracting action and event semantics from web text. In *AAAI Fall Symposium on Common-Sense Knowledge (CSK)*.

Temporal Expressions Extraction in SMS messages

Stéphanie Weiser **Louise-Amélie Cougnon** **Patrick Watrin**
CENTAL - Institut Langage et Communication - UCLouvain
1348 Louvain-la-Neuve, Belgium
{stephanie.weiser, louise-amelie.cougnon, patrick.watrin}@uclouvain.be

Abstract

This paper presents a tool for extracting and normalizing temporal expressions in SMS messages in order to automatically fill in an electronic calendar. The extraction process is based on a library of finite-state transducers that identify temporal structures and annotate the components needed for the time normalization task. An initial evaluation puts recall at 0.659 and precision at 0.795.

1 Introduction

In this study, the extraction of temporal information in SMS messages is regarded as a precondition to the development of an application for the construction of a calendar. This application includes the automatic analysis of meetings and the pre-filling of calendar events. We consider the language of temporal expression in SMS messages as a sublanguage which forms a finite subset of the whole language at the syntactic and lexical levels (Harris, 1968).

Most of the recent studies (Beaufort et al., 2010; Kobus et al., 2008; Aw et al., 2006) do not process SMS messages directly. They use a heavy preprocessing step in order to standardize the SMS script. We do not deny the relevance of the transliteration process for complex applications such as SMS messages vocalisation. However, within the framework of our project, we show that, for the extraction of temporal expressions, a normalization phase is not needed, as we tend to simply identify the boundaries of precise and particular surface structures.

Before exploring the extraction task (Section 3), we briefly introduce the corpus used (Section 2). The results of the evaluation we performed are outlined in Section 4, while Section 5 shows the prospects that emerge from this preliminary work.

2 SMS Corpus

2.1 Corpus-based study

The data used for this study is a corpus of 30,000 SMS messages (Fairon et al., 2006a) that were gathered following the strict *sms4science* collection methodology (Fairon et al., 2006b). *sms4science* is an international project that promotes the study of a substantial corpus of spontaneous text messages: users are asked to send a copy of text messages that they have already sent to a real addressee in a genuine communication situation. The 30,000 SMS messages corpus that constitutes the raw material for this study was collected in 2004 in the French-speaking part of Belgium; it was semi automatically anonymized and manually normalized[1] at the Université catholique de Louvain.

2.2 SMS Script Characteristics

We prefer not to talk about *SMS language* but about *SMS script* as it is not a new type of language but a new written practice through a new communication medium (Cougnon and Ledegen, 2010). This new practice shows various specificities, notably it seems to inhibit fear-related behaviour in writing — it erases traditional social, professional and academic demands. The addressee's physical absence, in addition to the delayed character of the media, encourages SMS users to play with language and to move away from standard language[2]. At a syntactical level, one would identify some similarities with French oral syntax such as the recurrent lack of *ne* negation marker and the absence of pronouns at the beginning of sentences. We follow a more nuanced path: it appears that these characteristics

[1] "SMS normalization consists in rewriting an SMS text using a more conventional spelling, in order to make it more readable for a human or for a machine" (Yvon, 2008).

[2] Standard language can be understood as a graphic and syntactic demand and/or as a register standard.

Proceedings of the Workshop on Information Extraction and Knowledge Acquisition, pages 41–44,
Hissar, Bulgaria, 16 September 2011.

are not related to the communication medium (oral/written) but to the communication situation (formal/casual) and are more related to register, in a Koch and Österreicher (1985) manner. Inspired by the theory of these authors, we consider there is a continuum between intimacy (*Nähesprache*) and distance (*Distanzsprache*) in the SMS communication model (Cougnon and Ledegen, 2010).

In addition to these variations to the norm, SMS script is also strongly influenced by social and regional features which increase the linguistic disparity (as in *On va au ciné* à soir/au soir/ce soir (in Canada/Belgium/France) - "We're going to the movies tonight"). Even though these variations are versatile, they form a finite set which can be formalised within a grammar.

3 Extraction of Temporal Expressions

In natural language processing, and particularly in the field of information retrieval and extraction, temporal expressions have been widely studied. The annotation (Pustejovsky et al., 2010; Bittar, 2010) as well as the extraction process (Weiser, 2010; Kevers, 2011) have often been addressed. Indeed, both are needed if we want to compute a date representation from the textual information (Pan and Hobbs, 2006).

These studies offer a wide range of solutions to automatically process temporal information, although they limit their experiments to standard language and don't take into account language variation. Nevertheless, some texts that could benefit from temporal analysis do not follow the norms of a standard language, notably an important part of CMC (Computer Mediated Communication) like e-mails, chats, social networks... In this study, we intend to determine if the methods used for standard language can be applied to more informal languages with specific characteristics, such as SMS script.

3.1 Typology of Temporal Expression

For an information extraction system, the typology of the data to be extracted is very important. We based this study on the typology developed by Kevers (2011) on standard language in which we selected the categories that are useful for our SMS temporal extraction purpose.

3.1.1 Existing Typology

Kevers (2011) classifies temporal information following four criteria that combine to give 16 categories: punctual or durative, absolute or relative, precise or fuzzy, unique or repetitive. For example, *Le 22 octobre 2010* is an expression which is punctual, absolute, precise and unique, whereas *Le 22 octobre 2010 vers 20h* (that has a different granularity) is punctual, absolute, fuzzy and unique.

This typology is very rich as it includes all types of temporal expressions found in standard (French) written language like dates, durations (*du 20 juin au 30 juillet* - "from June the 20th to July the 30th "), relative data (*le jour d'avant* "the previous day"), etc. However, not everything is useful for SMS temporal extraction.

3.1.2 Temporal Expressions to be Extracted for our Application

Our aim is to build an application to identify temporal information related to meetings or events in SMS messages. We do not need to extract past information (like *hier* - "yesterday" or *la semaine dernière* - "last week" or other information like *dors bien* ***cette nuit*** - "sleep well **tonight**"). More than that, as these expressions will serve as triggers for event extraction, the recognition of irrelevant sequences could lead to the identification of "false" candidates.

The information fundamental to this research and this application concerns meetings or events that can take place in an agenda. This is the only criterion that we used to determine the temporal expressions to extract (we call it the "calendar criterion"). The temporal expressions to be extracted can be:

- **a time:** *à 18h* - "at 6:00"; *de 14h à 18h* - "from 2 to 6"
- **a date:** *le 22 octobre* - "on October the 22nd"
- **a relative moment (day, part of day):** *aujourd'hui* - "today"; *maintenant* - "now"; *mardi* - "Tuesday"; *mardi prochain* - "next Tuesday"; *ce soir* - "tonight"; *dans 5 minutes* - "in 5 minutes"
- **an implicit expression:** *à mardi* - "see you on Tuesday"; *à demain* - "see you tomorrow".

According to the Kevers (2011) classification, the categories that are concerned by SMS messages events planning are PRPU (punctual, relative, precise, unique), DRPU (durative, relative, precise, unique) and PRFU (punctual, relative, fuzzy, unique). 13 categories from the original typology are not taken into account. We created a new category to deal with expressions such as *à demain* - "see you tomorrow" which imply that "something" will happen the next day. These expressions, which are typical of the dialogues found in SMS messages, were not dealt with by Kevers as the corpus he studied did not contain dialogues.

3.2 Sublanguage of Temporal Expressions in SMS

The study of Temporal Expressions in SMS messages has lead us to the observation that grammars which have been created for standard language can be applied to a specific sublanguage, at least for the temporal expressions in SMS messages.

3.2.1 Comparison with SMS Script

In order to compare temporal expressions in standard language with those in SMS script, we applied the temporal grammars developed by Kevers (2011) for standard French to the normalized version of an extract of the SMS corpus (1,000 SMS messages) and compared the original SMS form and the normalized form. We found that the syntax remains the same and that only the lexicon changes. A lot of variations are introduced in SMS script, but, concerning the sublanguage of temporal expressions, they only affect the form of the words and not the word order, the syntax or the semantics.

3.2.2 Adaptation of Existing Grammars - Lexical Characteristics

As we have just mentioned, the adaptation of existing grammars to extract temporal information in SMS concerns the lexical level. As SMS messages are well known for their lexical productivity, most of the common words are subject to variation. For example *demain* (tomorrow) is usually invariable but can take many forms in SMS: *2m1, dem1, dm1, dmain* ... In order to solve this problem we built a specialized lexicon in which each variation (*2m1*) is linked to a standard lemma (*demain*), a POS tag (*ADV* for adverb) and, in some cases, some semantic features (*Time*): {2m1,demain.ADV+Time}.

One may expect the lexicon to require constant updating, as it is intended to capture phenomena that rely on human linguistic creativity, which is potentially boundless. However, this theoretical assumption is refuted by our experiments which show that even if these forms vary consequently, they form a finite lexical set, respecting the closure property of sublanguages (Harris, 1968).

3.2.3 Resources Creation

Using the extracted expressions in normalized SMS messages, we have listed all the forms for all the words that appear in a temporal expression. This has lead to a preliminary dictionary composed of 177 forms, for 55 lemmas. This dictionary still needs to be extended but covers the main temporal expressions variants.

The grammar developed for standard French has been adapted: the invariable words have been lemmatized in order to match the variations listed in our dictionary, the sub-graphs that need to be applied have been selected and new sub-graphs have been created to cover the temporal expressions that are specific to SMS and do not appear in the original grammar (*à demain* - "see you tomorrow").

4 Evaluation

We performed an evaluation for the task of temporal expression extraction. We built an evaluation corpus and manually annotated the temporal expressions. Results in terms of precison and recall are provided in Section 4.2.

4.1 Evaluation Corpus

The evaluation corpus is composed of 442 SMS messages containing temporal expressions, following the "calendar criterion". Some SMS messages contain more than one temporal expression so the total number of temporal expressions is 666.

4.2 Results

For the task of temporal expression extraction, we obtained a recall of 0.659 and a precision of 0.795. Examples of well recognized expressions are, following the classification presented in Section 3.1.2 : *N'oubliez pas: ciné Pi* ***{ce soir,.ADV+Time+PRPU} {à 20H,.ADV+Time+PRPU}*** *aux locaux!* - "Don't forget: movie Pi tonight at 8:00 at the office!" (PRPU), *cela arrangeait pierre de venir voir asseliane {demain,.ADV+Time+PRPU}* ***{entre 11h et midi,.ADV+Time+DRPU}*** - "it would suit pierre to come and see asseliane tomorrow between 11:00 and noon" (DRPU), *on sera à la maison* ***{vers cinq h trente,.ADV+Time+PRFU}*** - "we'll be home around 5:30" (PRFU), *à demain* - "see you tomorrow"(new category). The reasons behind missing expressions or incomplete annotations are of three types. (i) The format of the expressions was not predicted and is not taken into account by the grammar, e.g. *à 8.30 - 9.00*; (ii) the variant of a word is missing from the dictionary, e.g. *dimanci* for *dimanche* - "Sunday"; (iii) there is a "mistake" in the SMS, e.g. ***un*** *peu près 15 minutes* instead of ***à*** *peu près 15 minutes* - "about 15 minutes". The results can easily be improved by working on the first two sources of errors (by extending grammars and dictionaries), while the third source of errors is more problematic, because they are really unpredictable.

5 Conclusion and Future Work

This preliminary study shows that the linguistic specificities of the SMS sublanguage of temporal expressions can be structured in order to eliminate the need for a transliteration process which can lead to errors that are difficult to deal with during the extraction process itself. This study points to numerous opportunities for future work as informal texts, such as informal texts such as SMS but also Tweets, chats, e-mails and Facebook status updates, become increasingly present and contain a lot of information that could be automatically processed.

We intend to apply this research to a calendar application that would find in an SMS all the data about events and time in order to open the calendar on the right date and help the user to fill it in. This approach suggests two complementary steps that we are currently working on:

- **Extracting the event itself**: it implies finding the subject (activity, event), the actants (in SMS, it is mostly the sender and the addressee), the time and place. On a linguistic level, we will try to find out if the properties of the sublanguage (a finite list of graphic and syntactic variations that can be formalized) can also be applied to the different items of events (place, subject, actants).
- **Importing the event in a calendar**: the important task in filling a calendar is to open it on the right date (and time). In order to do this, temporal expressions extracted from the SMS needs to be standardized and formalized in "calendar information" format.

References

AiTi Aw, Min Zhang, Juan Xiao, and Jian Su. 2006. A phrase-based statistical model for sms text normalization. In *Proceedings of the COLING/ACL 2006*, COLING-ACL '06, pages 33–40, Stroudsburg, PA, USA. Association for Computational Linguistics.

Richard Beaufort, Sophie Roekhaut, Louise-Amélie Cougnon, and Cédrick Fairon. 2010. A hybrid rule/model-based finite-state framework for normalizing SMS messages. In *Proceedings of ACL 2010*, pages 770–779.

André Bittar. 2010. *Building a TimeBank for French: A Reference Corpus Annotated According to the ISO-TimeML Standard.* Ph.D. thesis, Université Paris Diderot (Paris 7).

Louise-Amélie Cougnon and Gudrun Ledegen. 2010. C'est écrire comme je parle. Une étude comparatiste de variétés de français dans l'écrit sms. In M. Abecassis et G. Ledegen, editor, *Les voix des Français*, volume 2, Modern French Identities, 94, pages 39–57. Peter Lang.

Cédrick Fairon, Jean-René Klein, and Sébastien Paumier. 2006a. Le corpus SMS pour la science. Base de données de 30.000 SMS et logiciels de consultation. CD-Rom, Louvain-la-Neuve, P.U.Louvain, Cahiers du Cental, 3.2.

Cédrick Fairon, Jean-René Klein, and Sébastien Paumier. 2006b. Le langage SMS. *Louvain-la-Neuve, P.U.Louvain, Cahiers du Cental*, 3.1.

Zellig S. Harris. 1968. *Mathematical Structures of Language*. Wiley-Interscience.

Laurent Kevers. 2011. *Accès sémantique aux bases de données documentaires. Techniques symboliques de traitement automatique du langage pour l'indexation thématique et l'extraction d'informations temporelles.* Ph.D. thesis, Université Catholique de Louvain.

C. Kobus, F. Yvon, and G. Damnati. 2008. Normalizing SMS : are two metaphors better than one ? In *Proceedings of COLING 2008*, pages 441–448.

Peter Koch and Wulf Österreicher. 1985. Sprache der Nähe – Sprache der Distanz. Mündlichkeit und Schriftlichkeit im Spannungsfeld von Sprachtheorie und Sprachgeschichte. *Romanistisches Jahrbuch*, 36:15–43.

Feng Pan and Jerry R. Hobbs. 2006. Temporal arithmetic mixing months and days. In *In Proceedings of the 13th International Symposium on Temporal Representation and Reasoning (TIME)*, pages 212–217. IEEE Computer Society.

James Pustejovsky, Kiyong Lee, Harry Bunt, and Laurent Romary. 2010. ISO-TimeML: An International Standard for Semantic Annotation. In *LREC 2010*, Malta.

Stéphanie Weiser. 2010. *Repérage et typage d'expressions temporelles pour l'annotation sémantique automatique de pages Web - Application au e-tourisme*. Ph.D. thesis, Université Paris Ouest Nanterre la Défense.

François Yvon. 2008. Reorthography of SMS messages. Technical report, IMSI/CNRS, Orsay, France.

Bringing Multilingual Information Extraction to the User (invited talk)

Ralf Steinberger
European Commission Joint Research Centre
Ralf.Steinberger@jrc.ec.europa.eu

Abstract

The speaker will give an overview of how various text mining tools (information extraction, aggregation of multilingual information, document classification, trend analysis, and more) are combined in the Europe Media Monitor (EMM) family of applications to help users in their daily work. EMM was developed by the European Commission's Joint Research Centre (JRC), whose users include EU Institutions, national EU member state organisations, international organisations such as United Nations sub-organisations, and selected international partners (e.g. in the USA, in Canada and in China). The presentation will thus have an overview character rather than going into much technical detail. EMM applications are publicly accessible at http://emm.newsbrief.eu/overview.html. For scientific details and publications, see http://langtech.jrc.ec.europa.eu/.

Proceedings of the Workshop on Information Extraction and Knowledge Acquisition, page 45,
Hissar, Bulgaria, 16 September 2011.

Author Index